The Law Society's

INFORMATION TECHNOLOGY
DIRECTORY

SPD Ltd   Win95   16 bit
Responsive Systems Ltd
Law Computer Services   Ltd   Win95 16 bit + 32 bit
                                    Win95 32 bit
Kolvox
All Voice Computing   Win95   16 bit

THE LAW SOCIETY

113 Chancery Lane, London WC2A 1PL

© The Law Society 1996

ISBN 1 85328 406 8

Published by

THE LAW SOCIETY

113 Chancery Lane, London WC2A 1PL

Database typeset by BPC Whitefriars Ltd.
Printed and bound by BPC Wheatons Ltd., both members of the British Printing Company Ltd.

CONTENTS

In most firms, the decision to embark on an IT purchase is often taken at partner level but the actual work is done by the IT partner and by a member of staff given IT responsibility. Any purchase of IT has to be seen within the context of the partnership as a whole and, in particular, its business objectives. Given this, it is important that all partners take a healthy and enthusiastic interest in any IT project.

In this regard, we believe that the roles and responsibilities of all partners should be:

● to be aware of the business plans for the partnership and/or departments; particularly how the firm aims to distinguish itself in the market

● to have a high level appreciation as to how IT can benefit the working practices, competitiveness and profit of the firm

● to be involved in reviewing the specification of requirements prepared for the new IT system

● to assess the recommendations report on the chosen supplier to determine whether the original business objectives are being met

● to have some input to the implementation plan to ensure the timescales are realistic and that human resources can be made available

● to monitor the implementation and to raise any concerns

● to encourage and lead staff, by example, in the use of IT where appropriate

● to ensure staff are made available and receive sufficient training

IT is now recognised as a fundamental business tool. It can help reduce costs, improve productivity, enhance presentation and encourage a greater sharing of knowledge and information. However, the actual success of any IT project comes down to a few key factors:

● the partners' enthusiasm to grasp the opportunities provided by IT to benefit the firm as a whole

● the partners' appreciation that considerable effort and hard work has to be invested in the implementation process

● the partners' own encouragement to ensure that IT is only purchased to meet specific business objectives and not just because it is the "right" thing to do

● the firm continually researching what new IT developments can benefit the practice

This directory aims to provide guidance on how to choose and set up an IT system, and contains information provided by the main IT suppliers to lawyers in England and Wales. *This information has not been independently vetted, and any claim in an individual company profile should not be read as an endorsement by the Law Society.*

There are indexes for the types of system most often needed by solicitors, and suppliers are listed under each type of product with a cross reference to their main entries.

GETTING STARTED

This short overview is intended to guide law firms through the key considerations and recommended steps to use when contemplating major investment in Information Technology (IT). By major investment, we are talking about a firm-wide system or major complex application. The full process is not appropriate for smaller investments in, say, a word processing upgrade or choice of spreadsheet, nor is it appropriate for hardware upgrades only, although firms may find some of the guidelines and concepts helpful.

These guidelines are supported by a number of Law Society Technical Factsheets, which appear before the product indexes. These will be periodically updated to reflect the pace of change in the IT industry, and are available from the Law Society's IT adviser.

1. LINKING INFORMATION TECHNOLOGY TO BUSINESS NEEDS

The market for legal services is influenced by a number of external factors (i.e. outside the control of an individual law firm) including:

- changing and increasing demands of clients
- increased competition between law firms and other suppliers of traditional legal services
- legislative change
- the pace of technological change

The changing market poses threats to all law firms, who can no longer rely on their traditional clients and services to provide a steady income.

It is within this environment that firms need to consider how they are going to exploit IT.

IT can be used in one of two ways:

- to automate existing processes or to update obsolete technology
- to maximise business benefit by changing the way that lawyers work

Many firms can get caught in the cycle of upgrading systems with new technology without new thinking.

Systems selected in this way may not make the best use of limited financial and staff resources.

The existence of an up to date business plan is crucial to the IT decision. If the firm is seeking to expand in size, merge with another practice, offer new services to existing clients, offer existing services to new clients, reduce overhead costs, improve financial management and attract bright young lawyers, then the systems selected need to support these objectives.

The IT strategy is a **framework** that sets out the goals and aspirations of the practice from the IT perspective. It forces the firm to think about how it will use and exploit IT for competitive advantage and how the market for legal services is likely to change in the next few years (the anticipated life of the systems being considered). Strategies need to be reassessed periodically (at least once a year), such is the pace of technical change and competition within the legal marketplace.

Simply put, the IT strategy addresses the following questions:

Where are we now?

This is a review of the current use of IT within the firm to identify the Strengths, Weaknesses, Opportunities and Threats (known as a SWOT Analysis) in terms of:

- the systems and facilities currently used
- how IT is managed
- the IT skills within the firm
- the costs of the existing systems
- the number of users

Where do we want to be?

This identifies the key tasks that must be done well (known as critical success factors) to meet the firm's business objectives and how IT can support the achievement and monitoring of these factors.

It will result in a list of potential projects (or groups of applications) each of which should be quantified in terms of cost, business benefit and business risk.

How do we get there?

This looks at the alternative ways of getting from where the firm is today (in its use of IT) to where it wants to be, paying due regard to the priorities, constraints and technical options available.

Once the best way forward has been determined, a more detailed plan for the implementation should be developed and agreed throughout the partnership.

This end result, the **IT Strategy**, should be the basis for all IT investment until such time as it is modified to reflect further change in the firm's strategy or major technological change.

Conclusions

If your firm does not have any business plans and a linked strategy for the use of IT, then you have no basis on which to judge the effectiveness of your resources committed to IT.

Every firm, whatever its size, should develop an IT strategy to support its business plans unless the proposed IT spend is, for a short term, justified business imperative.

If your firm feels unable to carry out the key steps in the development of an IT Strategy, then you should consider seeking the services of an IT consultant to assist you in this process.

Whatever the current use of computers by your firm, at least one person within the firm should be given a watching brief to regularly review how IT is being used by legal firms. This is best done by a combination of reading (e.g. IT sections within the legal press, Law Society factsheets) and viewing (e.g. at Exhibitions).

It is often only by seeing systems in action that the potential of IT for improving the way that legal work is done and improving the service provided to your clients can be assessed.

2. IDENTIFICATION OF DETAILED REQUIREMENTS

After having identified and agreed the priorities and objectives of the required systems to meet the needs of the practice (**IT Strategy**), the next stage is to identify in more detail the main features of the system(s), the facilities required and who will use them.

The features should be documented, both as a means of obtaining internal agreement as to the requirements and as a way of communicating the requirements to potential suppliers to enable them to give your firm a quotation for systems supply and support.

A recommended first step in identifying the features required is to concentrate on the information that you want the systems to store and produce. Break down the overall system first into a number of application areas. These can be specific (such as Accounting or Time Recording) or generic (such as Case Management or Lawyer Support systems).

The information required will be a mixture of statutory information and returns (e.g. to conform to Solicitors' Accounts Rules), internal information to aid the running of the firm (e.g. billings, debtors, work in progress, new clients), specific requirements according to the legal work being carried out, such as the production of the appropriate legal form, and, most importantly, the information that the client may request or that you need to be instantly available to handle client queries and produce client correspondence and bills.

You will also need to think about the methods to be used for communicating both within the firm and with clients and intermediaries. Most firms use a combination of post, DX, fax and telephone. There are now an increasing number of other electronic alternatives or ways of using facilities more efficiently. Many of these are now integral to "Office Suites" of programs that allow you to easily capture information from your legal applications.

In order to build up the requirements into a specification that can be used in discussions with potential suppliers, the firm will need to consider the impact of the new systems on their current organisation in terms of **who does what**, **where**, **when and why**.

One of the main advantages of fully integrated computer systems is the ability to share accurate information throughout the firm. Consideration needs to be given as to who would benefit from viewing and, possibly, updating information from a specific module. This will help in detailing which applications must share or pass information to other application areas. This is known as **systems integration**.

Such consideration will allow the computing hardware requirements to be identified. The number of users will also influence the cost of the software. A picture needs to be built up as to who **may** access the information and how many of these people **will** need to access it at any one time. This, in turn, will help to define how many printers may be required, of what type and where they will be best placed. Consideration also needs to be given to the likely increase in the volume of transactions passing through the systems. This could influence the sizing and technical architecture of the system.

Help with the "User Requirements"

Contact the Society for Computers and Law (SCL) (Tel: 0117 9237393) who have local branches and meetings where you can talk to other practitioners and find out about local consultants in your area.

Your local TEC will also have information about local consultants, and funding may be available through the DTI Business Links scheme administered by the TECs.

3. SELECTION OF APPROPRIATE IT SUPPLIER(S)

Having written down and internally agreed the main requirements in terms of software and hardware you will need to consider the factors (or criteria) for choosing a system supplier. You should also consider the degree of risk your firm is prepared to take, possibly by being an early user of a new product or legal application.

Few firms select solely on cost grounds, unless it is for a commodity item. Whilst a standard 486 Personal Computer (PC) may be considered a commodity item by a very large firm who have their own IT specialists, it is unlikely that a smaller firm would take the same view. The smaller firm is likely to want a maintenance contract on the PC, assistance in loading the software onto the PC, operator training in the use of hardware and software, assistance in the event of problems and the peace of mind that the system selected is from a reputable supplier using up-to-date technology.

How do we identify the potential system suppliers that best meet our requirements?

The legal market has a very large number of suppliers, particularly for basic Solicitors Accounting and Time Recording systems. There are 120 in this Directory. It is clearly impractical to approach all these suppliers. Company profiles in this Directory give an overview of each firm's activities, products and size of solicitors firms catered for.

There are a number of potential sources of information relating to potential suppliers; the most useful ones to consider are the trade press, exhibitions, supplier mailshots, recommendation from other firms and independent consultants.

Having considered the evaluation criteria, you may be able to reduce the numbers of potential suppliers considerably to, say, the top five that appear to meet your requirements, based upon telephone calls to potential suppliers. If you already have systems in place you may wish to reuse some of the equipment - this may point you to particular suppliers of networked PC systems rather than centralised Unix-based systems. Another major consideration can be the potential supplier's experience in data conversion from your old system to the new. This is an area in which your existing supplier should be at an advantage.

With recent moves towards open systems standards, it is becoming more feasible to mix and match applications from a number of suppliers (i.e. to obtain the "best of breed" and link them together). However there are other considerations, such as ease of support, and possible additional costs to make the link and keep it operational as each application is enhanced over time.

Many of the leading IT suppliers to the legal profession already have links to certain third party products such as WordPerfect and Word for word processing or, in the case of suppliers that specialise in Case Management applications for the fee earner, to Accounting system suppliers. Some Accounting system suppliers can offer a choice of databases, making it easier to link to third party products that use the same database.

Who will we involve in the decision making process?

It is important to involve as many people as possible in the selection process so that there is support for the new systems when they come to be implemented. It is advisable to involve secretarial, fee-earning and accounting staff in the specification and selection phases. Their input can be invaluable when it comes to planning the implementation of the new systems and the consideration of new methods of working to maximise the benefits.

What services will be required from the supplier?

This will depend on the types of systems being considered and the internal IT skills available within the firm. If you are going out to tender, these services need to be defined as they will influence the overall cost.

Do we need to go through a formal tendering process?

For all but the simplest application, this approach is recommended. Without a comparison of costs, how do you know that you are obtaining value for money? Without comparing features or ease of use, how can you judge whether the concepts of a particular system are right for your firm? This approach could be adopted for a single major complex application or for a firm-wide system. Parts of the process may also be applicable for simpler applications.

The tendering process is designed to capture the information relevant to your decision making process enabling you to make a like-for-like comparison between suppliers. The supplier response can be linked to the purchase and support contracts eventually made with the chosen supplier. It is a way of ensuring that both sides understand what is expected from the system and the services and/or internal resources that are to be provided by each side.

A two-stage process is recommended for evaluating and selecting suppliers:

- an initial evaluation based on tender responses (or information pulled together from supplier literature) in order to shortlist two or three suppliers for detailed evaluation
- a detailed evaluation involving systems demonstrations, detailed discussions, taking up user references and preliminary negotiations on terms and conditions

4. SYSTEMS IMPLEMENTATION

Discussions with the shortlisted suppliers should have identified the main implementation tasks and likely timescales for implementation. Once a contract has been signed with the chosen supplier, detailed implementation planning must take place. This is one of the most important but frequently ignored stages of the computer project.

Both supplier and law firm staff need to be assigned specific tasks. It is easy to underestimate the time needed for implementation, particularly when done in conjunction with normal fee earning or support work.

Close liaison with the supplier is recommended in determining the input required from each individual. Do not forget to allow extra time for contingencies, which undoubtedly will arise. The identification of staff resourcing and training needs are vital issues to address as early as possible.

Once the plan has been agreed by all, implementation can commence. It is recommended that regular implementation progress meetings are held both internally and with the chosen supplier throughout the implementation period.

Around six months after implementation has taken place, a post implementation review is recommended to establish whether the business objectives are being met, how efficiently the system is being used and whether further training is required.

5. ONGOING SYSTEMS MANAGEMENT

Whatever the size of firm, someone needs to manage the IT resources in a firm once the systems are in place. It is normal for a partner to be given overall responsibility for IT, but that partner will need to be supported, either on a full or part time basis, by other staff particularly in a number of routine tasks.

Finally, it should be re-emphasised that a firm's IT strategy is not a task done once every five years. Changes in the legal market and the increasing pace of technological change make it essential that the applicability of the strategy is reassessed at least once a year.

Both the partner responsible for IT and staff with IT responsibilities should be made aware of any changes in the firm's business direction so that they can contribute to the discussion as to how IT can help re-focus the business.

Computer Systems for Sole Practitioners and Small Firms

Christina Archbold

The Law Society does not recommend any specific hardware or software, but these notes are offered as guidance to help you make a decision. They are designed for the small firm (less than 20 staff).

Other Law Society Resources

These notes are a starting point. We are also in the process of developing more resources to help you with your IT requirements.

- IT Guidelines - these provide the "how" to start in detail - a sort of do-it-yourself consultant. FREE
- Factsheets - information on specific types of packages (e.g. accounting) with lists of what to look for. FREE
- Video - "No IT Please - We're Solicitors" - a recording of the session at last year's Solicitors' Conference - an amusing play showing how technology can really make a difference (available on loan now). This has proved useful for showing less than enthusiastic partners what is possible
- Discounted Software - we are entering into arrangements with two of the three major "generic" software suppliers (Lotus and Novell) to enable solicitors to buy their software at substantial discounts
- Discounted Hardware - we are also in the process of negotiating hardware discounts for the profession
- "High Street Starter Kit" - we have been working with some suppliers to put together a software suite for small practices just starting out on the legal IT road. There will be three "flavours" available based on software provided by the three major software companies - Lotus, Novell and Microsoft. These packages are being trialled at the moment in some law firms (if you would like to volunteer to be a guinea pig - let us know!). The final packages should be ready around September '96

For free guidelines, factsheets and further information on discounted products from the Law Society, please call 0171 320 5697.

The Computer Environment

As with most things in life, you get what you pay for. A good rule is to buy the best you can afford, rather than the cheapest you can find. There are certainly some "cheap" computers out there - but they are doubtless outdated (e.g. 386s). The minimum you should expect to spend on hardware and software for one machine is around £2,000. Attornies in the USA have a good rule of thumb - they say that, if you're spending $3,000 for a machine with software, you're probably getting something that will last three years. The printer is extra and the cost will rise if you want to network your machines.

Windows will soon be the dominant "graphical user interface", which means that you use a mouse to point and click the things you want to do - as opposed to using keyboard commands, although typing is still involved if you want to use the equipment for word processing. You can also use lots of software applications at the same time - moving from window to window (hence the name "Windows"). If you are starting afresh now - don't buy anything that isn't a Windows product. All new hardware automatically comes with a basic version of Windows.

Windows '95

In August '95 Microsoft launched a new version of Windows - Windows '95. This is essentially a new departure, because if you use Windows '95 you no longer need DOS. This means that "DOS is Dead" and that old programmes written for the DOS environment will rapidly become obsolete. So ensure that you get programmes that are designed for Windows or Windows '95. The pundits' advice is to wait for a while before upgrading from ordinary

Windows to Windows '95 - but if you are buying a new machine it will come with Windows '95 already installed. This is fine. The key message is if you are using ordinary Windows now you don't have to think about changing just yet, but if buying new - Windows '95 is OK.

INTEGRATION

Integration is at the heart of new office technology. A good integrated package means that the user does not have to know which particular piece of software is doing which particular task. Tell it to produce a document and it goes off and gets the word processor for you. If you want to produce a bill, it goes off and gets the accounts/time recording. The idea is that everything is centred around clients and their matters rather than around the particular piece of software you are using (e.g. the word processor). Some specialist legal suppliers have fully integrated packages like this based in Windows. Others put modules together according to their specific requirements.

"Multi-media" packages are also on the increase. This means that more and more software will start to incorporate video clips, graphic images and sound. At the moment multi-media applications are very expensive, but doubtless the cost will drop as the technology becomes cheaper. More and more resources are appearing in a "multi-media" format, particularly in the education/training area. If you have children you may have already seen some of the games that are available. It will not be long before these techniques are applied to business applications. Some of the large legal publishers are starting to produce multi-media legal resources on CD-ROMs (and the Law Society already produces a Directory of Expert Witnesses on CD-ROM). These applications do not use sound and video (yet), but a CD-ROM drive is essential.

NETWORKING

Networking (linking your computers and sharing information) takes you into a much bigger - and more expensive - arena than if you operate "stand-alone". Both approaches have their advantages and disadvantages. You should consider networking if you have two or more people wanting to share equipment, e.g. printers, documents or accounts. It is just about

viable for two or three people to share information on floppy disks, but I would always recommend networking if possible. To network effectively you will need the advice of a consultant and/or supplier. As a sole practitioner/small firm you may have staff that you feel need to share information on a regular basis. If, however, there is just you and a secretary you can probably survive without it - so long as you exercise strict version control on your documents!

Networking is a complicated topic and there are various ways of doing it. Put simply there are two levels:

- peer-to-peer
- client/server

As a small practice you will probably be more interested in **peer-to-peer** networking which is fine for up to 10 PCs. This enables you to share documents, view colleagues' diaries, make appointments and send electronic mail. This offers advantages when several people are working together on the same case, or if you and a colleague need to share information. Printers can also be shared so that you can print a document on your secretary's printer. To do this you will need a network card for each machine, cabling to link them together and software such as Windows for Workgroups. The problem with this approach is that if one machine fails for any reason the whole network goes down - you can't use any of the other machines until you fix the problem.

Client/server is appropriate for more than 10 PCs. This will require a bigger machine (file server) to sit in the middle of a network and hold all the information that everyone needs to access. It is still possible to store things that only you need on your own machine (the client). This sort of network can span several offices in different locations using telephone lines to make the link between them. At this level the physical task of managing a network will need someone from your staff to be trained - or a maintenance contract with someone to act as your "network administrator". This type of network is more "fault tolerant" than peer-to-peer - if one machine goes down the network will keep running. It is also easy to back up (copy) information, as you can organise it all to be in one place (on the server), and not scattered around different machines (as in peer-to-peer).

STAND-ALONE

Traditional IT wisdom decrees that you select your software first, and then decide on the hardware you need to run it. However, for a sole or small practice the following hardware specification will be more than ample to run a basic legal business system. If you are thinking about buying just one (or maybe two) computers for stand-alone or peer-to-peer networking you will need to get the following:

- A Pentium with at least 8MB of RAM (Random Access Memory). Multi-media applications need at least 16MB. Pentium is the trade name for what would have been the 586 and you should get it with as much RAM as you can afford. You may pay a little more now, but it will go some way to ensuring that the machine will support the next generation of software

- At least 500MB of hard drive. A hard drive (or hard disk) is where all your electronic files are stored when you switch the machine off. These include files that run programs as well as your data files (i.e. the documents that you produce)

- Multi-Media - more and more multi-media machines are appearing on the market. Buy one if you can afford it. At a very minimum make sure your machine has a CD-ROM drive that has as high a specification as you can afford. The other element that makes a machine "multi-media" is sound. This comes in the guise of a special "sound card" inside the machine and speakers. Whilst not an absolute business essential at the moment, it's only a matter of time before business applications will start talking to you

- A laser printer (between £300 and £500). It is very important to be aware of the difference between laser printers and "laser quality" inkjet printers, especially when you are using legal forms software. Ask about the cost of consumables for the printer, i.e. the cartridge. This can vary in price from around £35 to nearer £100 depending on the printer - a significant running cost to be borne in mind

- A modem. This is now essential. Communications software will come with it. You can get a modem either as a card that slots into your machine (and is not much bigger than a credit card) or as a separate stand-alone "box". Again, buy the fastest you can afford. 14,400 baud is the slowest you should consider, get 24,000 or higher if you can. This affects the speed at which you transmit things. As you will be using a telephone line and incurring telephone costs, the faster you can get on and off line the better.

You can also get a fax/modem which can do all the things an ordinary modem can do plus software that allows you to send faxes from your computer either to a fax machine, appearing as an ordinary fax on the fax machine at the other end, or straight into a computer at the other end. Faxes arriving directly onto a computer arrive as "images". This means that you cannot go into them directly and edit them, as you would a word processing document. However, it is possible to get some software for "optical character recognition" which will translate the image into an editable form

- Network cards and cabling if you want to link together

Applications

Bear in mind the comments about integration above.

Word processing

Any Windows-based package is good, e.g. Word for Windows from Microsoft, Word Pro from Lotus, WordPerfect for Windows (Novell). Please note that WordPerfect for Windows has a completely different "feel" from WordPerfect for DOS (that you may well have at the moment). You will still have to invest in training for your support staff to make the transition into the Windows environment so WordPerfect for Windows is not a cheaper option in this sense.

A word about compatibility

All good Windows word processors can translate documents produced on the more common word processors. For example, Word for Windows and Word Pro can easily read WordPerfect documents keeping most of the formatting in tact. You then save the document as a new Word/Word Pro document. If you have worries about this, ask the supplier to demonstrate how you do this using one of your own documents.

ACCOUNTS/TIME RECORDING

What to look for in a good legal accounting system

All suppliers say that their systems comply with the Law Society rules - and they probably do. However, below are some pointers that will help you decide how well the system can help you abide by the rules.

● **Bank Reconciliations**

Check how the system helps you do this. Is it possible to pull out the items in the cash book which have not been presented to the bank yet? With many systems you end up doing this manually - i.e. getting a print-out of the cash book and checking it off against your statement as there is no way of letting the system know what has been presented. Obviously it's better if the system allows you to know the true position at any one time and is geared up to help you do this.

A key account rule is reconciling what you owe to clients with the money you are holding. Will the system allow you to reconcile across numerous bank accounts (including client deposit accounts)? How does the system handle multiple client accounts?

How does the system handle the banking process? For example, if you put a number of items into the client account on one paying-in slip, this will appear as one item on your statement. However, it is likely that this is made up of a number of items on your client ledger (i.e. a number of cheques received on behalf of a number of different clients). Reconciliation requires that you are able to match the two. How does the system help you do this?

● **Deposit Interest Calculations**

Will the system allow you to calculate interest on the client accounts according to the Law Society threshold table (see Solicitors Accounts Manual, fifth edition, para 27.54) without having to input manually for each client? A good system will identify the matter and do this automatically for you - i.e. it will calculate the interest due depending on the current threshold as defined in the rules. Some systems claim to have this facility but actually only act as a glorified calculator, leaving you to do most of the work in identifying the matters that have interest due, etc.

● **Money in respect of Controlled Trusts**

For these accounts the thresholds do not apply and you must pay the client all the interest at the rate received. To do this easily your accounts system must be able to handle multiple rates of interest on all the accounts where you hold this sort of money. Ask how the system copes with this issue

● **Overdrawing the Client Account**

Some systems will not let you do this. Whilst this may seem a good thing in theory, a good system should allow you to do the postings that will overdraw the account but warn you to make the necessary transfers from the office account. Then your computer records are always a true and accurate record of what is going on

● **Legal Aid Money**

How does the system handle this? Does it allow you to allocate your receipts from the LAB directly to matters?

● **Disbursements**

You may want to bill your client for disbursements that you have yet to pay out on their behalf. How does the system cope with this? Some systems won't allow you to post unpaid disbursements and this can cause problems

● **Integration**

How well can the accounts package talk to the other applications you are using, e.g. your word processor? Ask what happens if you want to send a personalised letter to all your clients who have recently settled their bills in full within 30 days. How easily could this be done?

Whilst the above is not a definitive list of what to look for, it highlights some of the things that need to be done easily to facilitate your compliance with the Accounts Rules. A computer can be of enormous help, but if you find yourself having to duplicate things manually to do key tasks then it's not a good system.

NB: no computerised account system will be able to help you with your accounts if you do not have your manual procedures and processes in place and in working order. There will be endless problems and delays if you expect your computer supplier to come in and re-organise a shambles. A common complaint from suppliers is that they often end up teaching cashiers the basics of accounting and Law Society Rules before they can implement the system. This naturally slows down implementation and causes frustration all round. Make sure your manual system is well sorted out first and get expert advice if necessary; it will save you a lot of headaches.

OTHER APPLICATIONS

Other software to assist your practice is legion; a lot of it is designed to take you through typical processes (e.g. conveyancing) and help you through each step, producing the right document etc. Such applications are called Case Management systems in the legal IT world or "Work flow" in the wider IT world. They are supplied by specialist legal suppliers and the quality of the software is variable. If your budget allows consider:

● **Legal Forms**

Check that they are compatible with your word processor. If it's Windows-based there should be no problem

● **Client Database**

Good accounts packages have this at their heart (i.e. you can use the client information in the accounts package and add other peripheral information that will help you with such things as marketing)

● **Document Management**

This helps you organise your documents and find anything using a "keyword", thus greatly enhancing the value of your documents. It is possible to think "I did a lease like this a while ago" and find it very quickly and easily if you can remember a single word that would distinguish it. A very rudimentary form of this is available with Windows-based word processors, but it is not nearly as good as the real thing. Document management software essentially allows you to create your own "know-how" database as most of your legal knowledge and wisdom is invariably stored in a document somewhere

● **Full Know-how**

You can become as sophisticated as you like and add an "imaging" function to your document management. This means that you scan in paper-based documents and then index them for future reference. You can turn the images into text by using a program called OCR (Optical Character Recognition) and then the images become fully editable and searchable by using key words. With this in place it is possible to put all your legal knowledge, forms, precedents, magazine articles etc. at your (or your secretary's) finger tips

● **Document Assembly**

You can get software to help you "assemble" documents from standard clauses. There are various packages around to do wills and leases like this. Essentially, you answer key questions on screen and the program goes away and pulls together the relevant clauses based on the answers to the questions. It is also possible to create your own "document assembly" package by using a piece of software called "Hot Docs" (£150 approx.). This allows you to collect your favourite precedents and highlight the parts that change (e.g. the client's name or address or the date). You can then get the program to automatically replace these areas of the precedent with the correct details for your current matter. If you have complex leases or other documents Hot Docs can save you invaluable time and energy by going through them to make sure you have changed all the details

● **Contact Manager/Scheduler**

What you are looking for is something to help you manage your contacts with clients (which should help you provide even better quality client care) and make sure that you meet your critical deadlines. Software to help with these things can come on its own or as part of a wider package (case management or marketing). You may not want a full blown client database or case management system but, if you are working in Windows for Workgroups, "Scheduler+" comes as standard (i.e. at no extra cost) - so consider using it to manage your clients and/or matters

● **Voice Recognition**

The quality of this type of software is increasing in leaps and bounds and is now becoming something to consider. The idea is that you no longer have to use a keyboard, but that you can "talk" to your computer to both give dictation and also operate software. You will need a high specification computer with at least 16MB of RAM. (The basic minimum outlined above is 8MB - it is about £100 per 4MB of RAM.) See Michael Kaye's essay on page 27 for more information

● **Internet**

The Internet is a worldwide telecommunications network of computers. At the moment some 13 million computers are "on the Net" (or Web) and this is increasing daily - i.e. they have agreed to talk to each other by implementing a common protocol that allows people access to their machines. People and organisations are now starting to design information and services specifically for the Internet. This includes lots of law firms across the world. Some of the larger firms here in the UK have put information about themselves onto "home pages" - a sort of electronic marketing leaflet. Stories are starting to circulate about how people found clients using the Internet.

The Law Society has "home pages" (i.e. pages of information) on the Internet - you will find us at **http://www.lawsoc.org.uk.** We hope to develop this to become an invaluable source of information to sole practitioners and High Street firms. Come and visit us and make suggestions about what other things you'd like to see there

Getting Connected to the Net:

The basic idea is that your computer (using your modem) makes a local rate call to a POP (point of presence). This is usually a big machine

run by an Internet Provider. You sign in with passwords and then you can access your electronic mail and go out for a "surf" onto the Internet. You cannot access the Internet directly from your own PC - you have to go through one of the providers. The number of providers is growing every day. The usual deal is that you pay a small connection charge and then a monthly charge - somewhere between £5 and £20 a month - depending on the amount of services you want to use. Basic facilities such as electronic mail and the ability to explore the Internet should not cost more than £6 a month per user.

For more information about the Internet turn to the article by Delia Venables on page 23.

SUPPLIERS

These fall into two types:

● Specialist Legal Software suppliers
● "Generic" suppliers

With specialist legal software always look for a package that you think your granny could use with minimal explanation (if she knew anything about legal business). This will invariably involve the screen having pictures and words on it that make sense to you as a lawyer and which bear some resemblance to the way you work. If you can't make head-or-tail of what you're seeing, this is NOT your stupidity, it is probably old fashioned and out-of-date software. Needless to say - don't buy it. You might think this is common sense but some people do feel at a distinct disadvantage when under pressure from a salesman. Don't give in! If you don't understand it, say so! It's their duty to explain, not yours to be a computer expert. On the other hand, be reasonable. If you are too picky and take too much delight in embarrassing the salesman you won't get the co-operation and support you need. Try to think of your IT supplier as a long-term business partner and treat them accordingly. You should be aiming for a long-term and mutually beneficial relationship. Get someone you can work with - even better, someone you like.

However, this doesn't mean you have to buy all your IT from one supplier. Check their attitude to working with other suppliers who may have packages or modules you prefer. Whilst it is usually good to try to have only one supplier responsible for all your IT, so that when it goes wrong there is no room for buck passing, if you want to piece things together to suit your own specific requirement that's perfectly OK. It is not acceptable for suppliers to charge large amounts of money to convert information into a form that other packages from other suppliers can use. So find out their attitude to such things before you decide to become friends and *get it written into the contract!*

The basis of a good relationship is a good contract for supply. You must READ THE SMALL PRINT and make absolutely sure that you are getting what you think you are getting. If possible make sure that it also includes time scales for implementation. Specify a date that you want your system up and running and specify what happens if the deadline is not met. (I've spoken to a solicitor who is still trying to get an accounts package running 18 months later!) Specify in detail what you mean by "up and running". A reputable supplier will be happy to talk about these things and include them in a contract with reasonable clauses (check for the all encompassing "get-out").

Specialist suppliers will seek to do you a "total" solution - which includes hardware and all your software, including word processing (see "generic suppliers" below).

Generic suppliers

These are the high street dealers/mail order suppliers who will be able to supply you with Word for Windows, WordPro or WordPerfect at extremely competitive prices. If you really have little or nothing to spend consider getting one of the software "bundles", e.g. Microsoft Office, Lotus "Smartsuite" or WordPerfect Office. These are really very good value and come with word processing, spreadsheets, and sometimes database and electronic calendars, etc. These are standard business packages and not tailored for the legal office. All cost around £350. Microsoft Office Professional includes a database at around £500.

They will also be extremely competitive on hardware prices - but check the amount of RAM. As I said above, 8MB is the essential minimum but seriously consider getting more if you can afford it. The cheap prices quoted in magazines and newspapers are nearly always for 4MB. You can buy your hardware and software "off the peg" like this and it will probably be as cheap as you are likely to find. But again check your guarantees etc. and what the supplier will do in the event of breakdowns/faults. (Think of the sort of questions you would ask if you were buying a second hand car on behalf of a client. The same logic applies!) If you do this, there is nothing wrong with this approach.

IMPLEMENTATION ISSUES

Implementing IT for the first time (or upgrading) is not easy. Try to include everyone who will be involved in the use of IT in the decision making process. It may not be appropriate to consult them at every stage but it is important to consult staff before the supplier turns up with the boxes - otherwise they may resist the change.

Ensure that you have an implementation plan with who will do what by when clearly mapped out. Agree this with the supplier before you sign the contract for supply.

Training is a key issue. You must allow plenty of time and money for this, otherwise your efforts will be wasted. Ask suppliers what they are willing to provide and at what cost. Please don't expect to be able to get everything up and running overnight. At times it will not go smoothly - but the long term benefits far outweigh the initial problems. It has been said that training on specialist systems ought to double the cost of your implementation. This may seem hard to swallow, but I can't emphasise enough how important training really is.

Plan to give your secretary a refresher course after three and, maybe, six months - especially if she/he is not used to Windows-based software. Training need not cost the earth. For the generic packages (e.g. Word/ Ami Pro/Excel etc.) there are plenty of courses at colleges in the evenings (and sometimes day times). Commercial training comes in at around £250 a day and can be provided at their premises or yours. Failing this, think about investing in some good training books/videos. Your high street store will also be able to point you in the right direction.

If you are using a specialist legal supplier make sure adequate training is included as part of your contract. Make sure you know what cost is involved if this doesn't come free. Make sure you get User

Documentation - i.e. a manual to look things up in if you get stuck - as part of your deal. The quality of this manual will often be an informal indicator of the quality of the supplier.

Current documents/data

If you are already using a computer system, then you will want the information you already have on it transferred to the new system. This should be possible with most word processors, although with the older accounting packages anything could happen! Ask your supplier about this transfer, i.e. who will do it, how long it will take and how much it will cost. Please bear in mind that there will inevitably be a problem and at the very least you are likely to lose some formatting on your word processing documents. This is not the end of the world, but time will be needed to put them back into your own style.

Security and backup

You will need to ensure your information is regularly copied onto either disks or tape and stored in a safe place. This is essential. You should back up your information daily - and store the disks or tape somewhere else - i.e. at home. Security is also essential. Make sure that your computers are both physically safe (so don't leave the office unlocked at night) and also that the software has an appropriate level of security through the use of passwords. You will feel a lot better about things (and so will your clients) if you have taken these precautions and your PCs are stolen or damaged. Imagine what it would be like to reconstruct your accounting records from scratch if you lose your information and you do not have a backup.

Finance

The Law Society has organised finance from Medenta, a Lloyds Bowmaker subsidiary, for solicitors wanting to upgrade their IT. Telephone: 0800 442240.

KEY POINTS TO REMEMBER

- Plan ahead - if you don't know where you're going, you'll be lost when you get there!
- Involve everyone in your IT plans - and keep them involved
- Use a reputable consultant to help you plan and implement if you can afford it, or buy our IT Guidelines (the DIY consultant)
- Buy Windows products and steer clear of DOS packages
- Any word processor is fine - so long as it's designed for Windows
- Network your machines if you can, and go on the Internet
- Buy the best you can afford, not the cheapest you can find
- Read The Small Print In Your Supply Contract.
- If you don't ask for what you want, you won't get it. Make sure that your expectations and your supplier's are the same
- Training is vital for success

Finally...

Remember that IT is for life. Once you have made a start, there is an ongoing cost of ownership. This means a commitment to upgrading and training as and when necessary as well as simple things like new cartridges for your laser printer. The technology is improving in leaps and bounds and once you have entered the race, you will need to keep up. However, the positive side of this is that you will also stay competitive.

Please contact me if you have any questions. If you can't get through and have specific questions - please leave them as part of the message and I will get back to you.

Christina Archbold
IT Adviser
The Law Society
Voice: 0171 320 5697
Fax: 0171 320 5918
E-mail:cea@lawsoc.org.uk

USING IT TRAINERS

Jane Dudman

IT training is an area that is all too often overlooked when companies are buying software. But ensuring that staff are fully trained and able to use new systems to their full potential is a vital part of getting the best out of technology investment, and should be included as an essential part of the process of introducing new technology.

A glance at any specialist IT magazine will highlight the number of companies now in the business of selling training. Choosing the right options can be difficult, but, as with any purchasing process, it is important to clarify your requirements.

The first question a law firm, particularly a smaller firm which is less easily able to spare staff time on expensive computer training courses, must ask is why it should bother with training at all.

It could be argued that most software packages have developed considerably since the days when they ran on dumb terminals. Now, most PC-based software contains a good deal of built-in help. Graphical user interfaces are supposedly easy to use and self-explanatory, and many people will already be familiar with using computers and could be expected to become familiar relatively quickly with new software, particularly standard packages carrying out everyday tasks like word processing or even simple accounting.

These arguments become less convincing when considering more complex systems, such as specialised packages for handling legal documents, or software for handling case notes. There is no reason why someone well versed in handling legal documents and keeping track of them manually by using a paper filing system and some kind of card index, should suddenly be able to transfer those skills to the unfamiliar environment of a PC and a keyboard.

Whether looking at relatively straightforward office tasks, such as writing letters, or more specialised aspects of the legal business, it is necessary to take a step back and ask why the process is being computerised in the first place.

According to Peter Labrow, marketing manager of computer training specialist P&P Training, the answer is that companies invest in IT systems because they believe they will bring some benefit. From that premise, Labrow argues that these benefits will be gained faster if those who are to use the new systems get proper training.

"Law firms don't want to waste time," he comments. "Staff will spend time getting to grips with new systems, and while they could well grasp the basics in a day or two, it could take months to become really familiar with a package. Training gives a faster route to that knowledge."

Labrow adds that another benefit of training is that people learn the most effective ways to do things using their new system: "Most modern software allows the user a number of ways to do particular functions," he comments. "Training can ensure that users learn the right way to use packages."

As an example, Labrow highlights the differences between Windows 3.1 and Windows '95. He says if someone familiar with Windows 3.1 sits down in front of Windows '95 and is left alone to begin using the package, they will automatically use the procedures from the more familiar environment, and this will mean that to start up a program, they will look for the familiar Program Manager function and ignore the start button in the bottom left-hand corner of the Windows '95 screen.

"A manager could come back, see that person working perfectly happily in an application such as Word, and believe they understand the new software," says Labrow. "In fact, that person has just taken six steps to get into Word where a single step would have done. They've used good logic, and got where they need to be, but they haven't used the short cuts."

This may seem incidental, but getting the best use out of a system means knowing how to use it as efficiently as possible. After all, if staff spent half-an-hour every morning steaming open the post, it would soon be pointed out that it is quicker and simpler to use a paper-knife.

Another important consideration is the amount of time staff will have to spent supporting one another when a new system is installed. "Training removes the need for people to support each other," explains Labrow. "If you don't train people, those who have picked up a new system faster are slowed down in having to answer their colleagues' queries. It's a hidden support cost."

Labrow believes that all these factors apply with equal force whether the new system is a word processing package for administrative staff or a more specialised piece of legal software. "The benefits of training apply just as much to the high fee earners," he says. "In fact, more so, because they tend to have less time to invest, and without training they run the risk of trying something and becoming disillusioned with it. The system is then not used at all, and is a waste of investment."

Once convinced of the value of training, the next step is to choose the most effective training method, taking into account the type of software that is to be installed and the existing experience of the staff who are to use it.

There are many choices available, each with their own advantages and disadvantages.

One option is to send staff out of the office for training on one of the many group courses run by specialist IT trainers covering particular packages, usually run over one or two days. The advantage of this is that being out of the office enables staff to concentrate on the task of learning, with fewer distractions, and they will usually gain a considerable knowledge of the overall functions of the particular software. One potential disadvantage is that use of the package is not directly related to the staff member's specific needs back in their own office, although properly briefed trainers will attempt to ensure there is some attention to this topic.

Alternatively, an IT trainer can run a course in an organisation's own offices. This has the benefit of being tailored to the particular needs of the organisation and its staff, but tends to be used more by larger companies who will have enough staff to be trained at any one time to make this approach cost-effective, and who will tend to have the resources to set up a training room. One disadvantage of this approach is that people on a course in their own company tend to be distracted

more easily, popping out during breaks to see to urgent phone calls and so on.

In the 1980s, there was considerable interest in the development of computer-based training (CBT) methods, mainly because it was seen as more efficient and flexible for people to be able to train themselves in new software, at their own pace, using interactive CBT packages. It would also be cheaper, since it would cut out the use of expensive, classroom-based trainers.

The idea failed to take off, largely because the CBT products that were produced tended to be slow and uninteresting, and were not tailored to individual users' needs.

Ron Orme, divisional director of Parity Training, says CBT is boring because it is written for standard packages and simply goes through the package function by function. "It's just like reading a manual, except that with a manual at least you can flick ahead a few pages if you get to a bit you already know," he says. Orme believes that CBT will take off once it can provide a bespoke package, relating the software functions to the real job for which a person has to use them.

This is some way off yet, given that at the moment the cheapest bespoke CBT software still costs £8,000 an hour. But a computer-based approach to training is coming back into fashion, both as the software becomes more flexible and the hardware on which to run it becomes more powerful. Today's PCs are more powerful than machines of a decade ago and often have multi-media capabilities as standard - important in providing true interactive functionality.

CBT is now seen as having an important potential role within an overall approach to training, rather than simply replacing classroom-based training wholesale. When considering CBT, however, some caution is necessary. Buying a CBT package is much cheaper than buying classroom training, and a self-study course in a well-known application such as Word could cost as little as half as much as a classroom-based course, with the added advantage that it can be passed on from one staff member to another as necessary, which is of course very appealing. Spending £3,000 on a CBT package that can be used to train 10 people looks like a cost-effective purchase when it could cost up to £30,000 to train the same people in a classroom.

Organisations need to think carefully about whether such an approach really will provide value for money. Many IT trainers point out that without providing a solid training framework for the use of CBT, such packages can end up gathering dust on an office shelf. While one of the key advantages of a self-study course is its flexibility, enabling the user to learn at their own pace, this can mean that unless people are very well-motivated, sitting down with a piece of CBT software can easily slip to the end of the list of priorities in what is often already a busy schedule.

Despite these drawbacks, CBT can be a useful part of an overall training programme, according to many IT training companies. A number of training companies, including Learning Tree, Wave Technologies and SHL, have recently released training courses featuring CBT integrated with classroom-based training, and such companies agree that the integrated approach can provide an excellent and cost-effective training programme, particularly now that people in general are more familiar with computers.

Bob Woodland, managing director of SHL, for instance, says customers want to have CBT as part of an overall training programme, while David Pardo, UK managing director of Learning Tree, agrees that the training market has reached a level of sophistication where CBT can be accepted as a complement to existing courses, rather than an alternative.

Training company P&P uses self-study packages when training staff in more technical IT areas, enabling it to ensure that people have reached a minimum standard of knowledge before going on a more detailed, classroom-based course. And such technical staff are more likely, says the company, to be comfortable with computer-aided learning. Interest in the Internet is fuelling the rise of another training method: online training.

It is an area that software giant Microsoft is keen to develop. Last year, when it launched its Windows '95 package, the company also launched the Microsoft Online Institute, which uses Microsoft Network to combine a CBT self-study package with an online tutor system. The Online Institute is mainly aimed at those within the IT business who want to gain Microsoft's own Certified Professional qualification, and who are generally at ease with the Institute's combination of self-study and online access.

Microsoft is working with other companies to encourage the production of CBT packages and has set up an approvals programme for CBT software. It also emphasises the need for a flexible approach to self-study training, using a range of media from books and videos to CBT packages on CD-ROM as well as online facilities.

Training company Peritas has worked closely with Microsoft on the Online Institute and has also launched its own online training service. According to Peritas managing director Paul Butler, online training has tremendous potential and could open up considerable new opportunities for training companies and their customers.

Butler says the latest online services combine CBT materials with tutorial support via the Internet, giving the flexibility of the self-study approach but with the added benefits of one-to-one tutorial advice. He predicts a big boom in online training in the next few years and says his own company has already seen the difference that such an approach can make. "We are providing training for people in places like Hong Kong that we would not have been able to provide except via online services," comments Butler.

The average UK law firm may not yet envisage getting its staff trained via the Internet, but such training methods are certain to become more commonplace - and more cost-effective - as use of the Internet continues to grow.

In the meantime, organisations have to attempt not only to pick a suitable training medium, but also a suitable training company.

Steven Schmidt is business manager for education services at German software company Software AG and has just been appointed chairman of the Computing Education Management Association (Cedma) in Europe. Cedma was set up in 1994 by hardware and software vendors that provide training for their customers, and its stated aim is to promote practical and commercially beneficial best practices within the European IT education and training sector. Cedma's 23 corporate members include major names such as IBM, Microsoft, Lotus, Informix and Oracle.

Schmidt says in times of recession training is often the first budget to be cut by customers. Cedma's aim, he says, is to make organisations realise that training can, in fact, play a key economic role in improving company performance.

"In an age of continuing belt-tightening, every organisation has to ask itself what price IT training?" says Schmidt. "That is, they have to ask what will happen if they don't train staff in these areas and it is apparent that the first thing is that it takes longer to get things done. Without a rudimentary set of skills you can't set anyone down in front of even a relatively straightforward piece of software and expect them to be able to get on with a piece of work right away."

Schmidt acknowledges that many organisations, particularly smaller companies, do find the price of IT training an issue. "It is a difficulty," he says. "Price is a major influence, particularly with the emergence of new training technologies, such as CBT. But the whole idea is to ensure that customers do not ignore training as an essential part of implementing a system."

Cedma has produced a white paper outlining some of the major issues in considering IT training, and Schmidt also has advice on how to choose an IT trainer.

He says it is important to find out what the training company's own attitude towards training is. "Look for a company with credentials and ask what sort of training it provides for its trainers," he comments. "Do its trainers have any professional certification in relevant skills such as delivery skills and managing classrooms?"

Schmidt also suggests that customers should see if their potential training supplier has met such standards as the ISO 9001 quality standard for business procedures.

Finally, he suggests those buying training should ensure their potential supplier possesses the relevant proprietary qualifications from product vendors. "Major companies such as Microsoft, Lotus and Software AG have proprietary certificates in their product ranges. To gain such a certificate, people have to sit down and do an exam, and are tested on their basic skills and knowledge of the particular product. It is important that a training company should have such specialist knowledge, so although these are proprietary certificates, they do provide a valuable guide as to the skill levels of the training company," comments Schmidt.

Once a training company has been chosen, and the right mix of training materials agreed, organisations will want to ensure they are getting the most out of their investment in training.

Again, the key task is to define requirements clearly and measure results against them. Requirements will differ widely, not always according to the software being used, but according to who is using it and in what way. For instance, major City corporate law firm Wild Sapte has installed a PC-based network on which the major application is word processing. This sounds straightforward enough - but Wild Sapte runs a 24-hour-a-day operation, in which million-pound contracts are being worked on through the night.

Two things were therefore vital when the firm was implementing its new system: it had to be completely reliable, since the IT team would not be on hand at four in the morning, and the emphasis was on making the system as easy as possible for high fee-earning lawyers to use.

Today's PC applications, with their graphical user interfaces, are easier to use than the character-based dumb screens many of them replace. But the additional functionality that comes with powerful PCs also means that users have more opportunities to go wrong, so proper training becomes even more important, particularly in smaller firms that are unlikely to be able to afford a dedicated IT team.

But one of the biggest motivators in ensuring IT training is effective is ensuring all staff understand the potential benefits of the system. Since this should have been a fundamental part of the purchasing process, it should be a relatively straightforward task, but it is surprising how often technical champions within organisations fail to communicate this important point. No-one gets the best out of a system they feel has been forced on them for some vague idea that technology means progress.

Firms can avoid these pitfalls by ensuring staff at all levels understand why a new system is being brought in, and what it will be able to do. Building training costs into the project from the start will also go a long way towards avoiding expensive delays and mistakes.

THE INTERNET - AN OVERVIEW

Delia Venables

What is it?

The Internet is a fast growing global network of computers which are connected to each other and which share information. It enables users to communicate and share ideas with other people on an international basis.

In practical terms, the Internet allows a lawyer with a computer and a modem to communicate with businesses, clients and potential clients in this country and abroad and also to access a number of sources of information of legal and commercial interest.

Why get involved now?

A solicitor could well feel that there are already many other ways to communicate with people and to find information and perhaps there is no need to get involved with the Internet, just yet.

But there are good reasons for getting to grips with the topic now:

- All large businesses and many smaller ones are already on the Internet and will expect their legal advisors to know what they are talking about
- Larger institutional clients are already wanting to transfer new work to their lawyers and to obtain up to date information on the work already being handled, via the Internet
- Many areas of law, including defamation, copyright, intellectual property, the music and entertainment business and electronic commerce, now demand an understanding of Internet issues
- Potential "ordinary" private clients are also accessing the Internet in increasing numbers and may well, over a period of time, use the Internet to find a lawyer

What you need to get on the Internet

- An IBM compatible personal computer, preferably a Pentium (or at least a 486) and 8 megabytes of memory, running Windows or Windows '95. Apple Macs are just as good but are not so widely used in the legal market. A printer is also essential
- A modem of at least 14,400 bits per second speed and preferably 28,800
- A dedicated telephone line (i.e. not part of a switchboard)
- Basic computer experience. You have to enjoy sitting in front of a computer and possess basic computer skills - otherwise the whole thing will be torture
- A service provider, for example, Pipex (Tel: 0500 474739), CompuServe (Tel: 0800 289378), Microsoft (Tel: 0345 002 2000) or Demon (Tel: 0181 371 1234)

These companies provide you with the software you need and give you the basic connection to the Internet (i.e. the number you dial in to). They also assist you (via e-mail) if you get into difficulties. There is very fierce competition amongst them at the moment and charges vary widely, with initial free offers making the choice even more difficult.

My own view is that you want a service provider which:

- Aims at the business market rather than the mainly domestic one
- Offers unlimited access once the basic charge has been paid (no hourly access charge)
- Provides all the Internet software you need, including a piece of software called "Netscape"
- Offers a local "Point of Presence", i.e. a local phone number for your basic connection

You will need to check all these points with any potential service provider. Although not the cheapest, Pipex satisfies these four criteria (the fourth one to the 85% level - which is as good as or better than anyone else). Pipex charges £50 for the initial set up and then £15 per month.

As well as the service providers with national coverage, there are often local companies providing a more personal service. They are well worth considering.

E-mail

One of the most important, and useful, apects of the Internet is the ability to send messages across the world, in minutes, for virtually no cost. When you join the Internet, you are generally provided with an e-mail address automatically. This e-mail address identifies a little piece of space reserved for you on your service provider's computer which is used to store the messages sent to you. E-mail addresses look like this: http://www.lawsoc.org.uk.

To send or receive a message, you dial in to your service provider from your personal computer and collect (read) your mail. You can print it, or delete it, or reply to it, or send it on to someone else. Messages reach their destination, anywhere in the world, in minutes and generally cost you nothing except for the phone costs of the short time you are online and sending the message - often just a few seconds. You can prepare the message offline, i.e. whilst not on the telephone line, to keep costs down. Messages can have whole files (i.e. documents in electronic form) attached which can be read by the recipient and then word processed like any other document.

Newsgroups

Much of the journalistic interest in newsgroups stems from the fact that most of the pornography on the Internet is located there. However, there are tens of thousands of newsgroups which are *not* pornographic! Basically, they are a forum for the sharing of information and for carrying on a discussion on particular topics.

These newsgroups are sometimes also called "Usenet" groups or bulletin board services, depending on the software used to access them, and some of them can be limited to particular service providers or groups.

The World Wide Web

In many contexts (particularly commercial ones) the World Wide Web is becoming synonymous with the Internet and the two terms are often now used interchangeably. The web is a means of presenting information which allows pictures and graphics to be included and which also allows "hyperlinks", i.e. the ability to follow up a reference in a text or a picture to find additional layers of information.

You use a mouse to choose your options and, in theory at least, pictures, sound clips and even video clips can be located and shown on your screen. To access the web in this way requires special programs called "browsers", of which the best known is called Netscape - this is the one to have if you possibly can.

What's on it for lawyers?

It is true that most legal material is still USA based. It is also the case that, for a serious legal search on statute or case law, or law reports and commentaries, Lexis, Lawtel, Context or LINK (which are specifically legal online services) would provide more comprehensive and reliable material than the Internet.

However, the material available is growing all the time and here are some key sources in the UK.

The Law Society's home pages provide some invaluable links to worldwide legal resources. There are plans to develop this site further.

Legalease, whose publications include the *Legal 500*, *Law Firms in Europe*, *Legal Business* and *UK Legal Times*, and who also run the LINK service for lawyers, have now stolen a march on all other legal publishers with their new presentation on the Internet. They have placed the *Legal 500* on the Internet, with pages covering the specialisations of each firm, their size, partners and addresses. In addition, there is a parallel presentation of European lawyers. There is also a set of commentaries on current legal topics on their pages.

University of Southampton Law School has provided an index of UK official publications.

The Society for Computers and Law has set up a site with information about the society, the officers, events and meetings, and some topics of current interest.

Court on the Web provides information on how the British legal system works, with information on likely costs and the possibility of getting legal aid. This is intended for non-lawyers.

Legal aid availability is described in considerable detail on the government's pages, again intended for the ordinary citizen.

There is a newsgroup called **news:uk.legal** although this does not seem to contain a great deal of interest, however, being rather erratic in content.

A series of "**Collaborative Open Groups**" have been set up by the government, including a group to cover legal topics. These groups are really "mailing lists" for which you register (the instructions are provided on the web page) and then await messages which will be delivered to your e-mail address. Each person registered can contribute to the discussion in hand, or initiate a new discussion. The legal group has lately been discussing the copyright of government materials, data protection, copyright and encryption.

The full text of Lord Woolf's report *Access to Justice* has been put on the Internet.

Indiana University School of Law at Bloomington, USA, provides a large set of pointers to legal resources around the world, including search tools and lists of material by subject and by source.

The University of Newcastle has started an Internet journal of current legal issues.

The Universities of Warwick and Strathclyde are producing a new *Journal of Information, Law and Technology.*

A Short Cut is available at **http://www.venables.co.uk/legal/welcome.htm**. This is a set of web pages which I have set up myself. You will find here hyperlinks to all the legal sites described above and many more. There is also a list of firms of solicitors and barristers who have presented their own information on the web with direct links to the pages concerned, and information about software, courses and consultancy services aimed at the legal market.

Are you on the Internet?

If you answer "yes" to this question, it could mean several different things.

- It could mean that you have a connection to the Internet, as described above, and that you log on from time to time to collect your e-mail and "surf" the web
- It could mean that someone else (probably Legalease) has put your information on the Internet as part of a register of major firms, with basic information about address, partners, and work specialisations
- It could mean that you have set up your own web pages containing your own basic information

which acts as a sort of electronic shop window for the passing world

It is the third of these three categories which is the most interesting and demanding. To do this you need to "write" your pages in a particular language called Hyper Text Markup Language (HTML) and store these on your service provider's computer. There are a number of companies and freelancers around at the moment who can assist with this process, i.e. "HTML Authoring".

As well as writing your pages, you have to "rent" space on a computer, generally at your service provider, to store them and make them available to the world at large. This is quite cheap - typically, only £200 a year. In some cases (as with Pipex at the time of writing) space is provided free as part of a current sales promotion.

You may also wish to set up and register your "domain name", i.e. the part of the address which gives your brand image, like Clifford Chance or Allen & Overy. A great deal of commercial interest is being generated in this topic and it is a case of "first come first served" with the bodies that carry out the registration. Registering a domain costs around £200 and involves a certain amount of admin. and waiting around. Your service provider should be able to assist with this.

Then, of course, you have to know what you want to say. Are you talking to big business or ordinary people? Are you interested in specific markets, like engineering or the music industry? Are you trying to be informative, or funny, or dignified or clever?

As of May 1996, there were only around 40 UK firms who have actually set up their own web sites. In addition, several groups have done so, including LawNet, Law Group and ALeRT.

What are the alternatives to the Internet?

Finally, it is worth noting the alternative communications systems which are available to legal UK users. It may be that you do not need the Internet at all (at least for the moment).

LINK is the most widely used of all online services for lawyers. It provides e-mail within the LINK community, transfer of documents in most word processing formats and discussion groups on legal and technology subjects. There are also many legal articles and law reports available and a daily legal update. Most of these services are free.

LINK charges for certain additional services, such as corporate mail boxes, private discussion groups, Dun & Bradstreet credit checks, company formations, trademark searches, Laserform downloading, requests for Lexis searches, and a gateway to e-mail on the Internet. Although originally set up as a separate legal online service, the latest news is that LINK is moving its information onto the Internet itself.

LIX is another closed communications system for lawyers. It is a "point to point" service, i.e. no intermediary is required. Thus, when you send a LIX message, you send it direct to the recipient (like a fax) and the recipient actually gets it at the same time. All standard word processing formats are supported and encryption is available for documents that are particularly sensitive. There are also discussion groups.

LIX offers Royal Courts of Justice, Crown Courts and County Court listings, with a direct and selected service available (in other words, the required listings just "come in" to your firm without daily log-ins or requests).

LEXIS is the long established specialist online research tool. There is full text access to more than 9 million cases, including 88,000 British ones. All Public General Acts are available in amended form and there is a great deal of material from the USA and other jurisdictions. Nexis is the more recently developed service, providing users with a library of international news and business information. There is also a service called "Lexis Direct" by which Lexis researchers do the online work.

LAWTEL provides an extensive database of law report digests and case summaries. There is a daily update and a comprehensive digest of all the major law reports as well as unreported cases. There is also a statutory database with details on codified legislation, Bills currently progressing through Parliament, and Green and White Papers.

CONTEXT is not really an online service at all - it is primarily a CD-ROM publisher of legal materials. However, these two technologies (communications and CD-ROM) are essentially developing in parallel and, in some cases, it can be more efficient to have a CD-ROM in the library than to go online to one of the other services.

Context make a speciality of European law and European Union topics, as well as statutory instruments, parliamentary developments and Weekly Law Reports of this country. Although basically a CD-ROM publisher, there is also an updating service online for recent updates, thus really "closing the circle" between the two lines of development.

Delia Venables *is an independent computer consultant specialising in the needs of the legal profession. She has recently written the* Guide to the Internet for Lawyers *and also produces the bi-monthly* Internet Newsletter for Lawyers.

She can be contacted on 01273 472424 or delia@ venables.co.uk. Her own Internet site is at http:// www.venables.co.uk/legal/welcome.htm.

COMPUTER VOICE RECOGNITION

Michael Kaye

Computer voice recognition, the ability of a computer to receive dictation or commands given by voice rather than keyboard, has now become a practical reality for every office. The potential cost savings are so obvious that they need no explanation. The only problem is not whether to buy but when and which of the competing products to buy.

The products

There are currently three major systems, with other innovative and specialist products on the drawing board beginning to come onto the market.

The three major systems currently available are Dragon Dictate, Kurzweil Voice and IBM VoiceType. Dragon and Kurzweil are very similar and have the immense initial advantage of running within the word processor or other applications in use. After a short period of initial voice training of the system to the idiosyncrasies of the user's voice, the user is able to dictate directly to the word processor, and then by voice to command the word processor to format and subsequently print the document. The standard of voice recognition improves through use as the systems learn more and more about the way in which the user speaks and uses words.

The major disadvantage to using these two similar systems is not immediately apparent to a potential buyer on seeing them demonstrated. Quite simply if during dictation a word is incorrectly interpreted then within a very short period of time that word *must* be corrected to avoid the user's own personal speech module being updated with the mistake. The effect of this problem is that, in dictating something that is quite long and complex, the user must not only think about what he is about to say but also watch the words that he has just said appear, after a slight delay, on the screen. The overall effect is confusing and while the system works extremely well for standard dictation, complex matters are made more difficult by having to constantly watch for and correct errors, thereby breaking the user's train of thought.

The IBM system came to the market after Dragon and, while there are many similarities, the document production process is different and it is widely accepted that initial word recognition is better, although it is fair to say that each of the different systems has its own aficionados. The system was initially designed to run under IBM's own operating system, OS/2, although the sheer power of Microsoft in the market and the popularity of Windows as an operating system made it a commercial necessity for IBM to bring out a Windows version of its program. The IBM VoiceType system is priced competitively with the Dragon and Kurzweil systems and includes an additional board which is plugged into the back of the computer and which contains a separate processor often more powerful than the computer's main processor. The greater accuracy of voice recognition of the IBM system relies upon this additional power and accuracy is enhanced by a built-in grammar checker that will, for example, allow the dictation of such sentences as, "Are you their mother?" and "Are you there, mother?" to be dictated and spelt correctly. The user of the Dragon type system will have to amend the spelling of either "their" or "there" in the example given.

The major disadvantage of the IBM VoiceType system against its main competitors is that words are spoken into the VoiceType program window rather than directly into the word processor. But, with the modern ability of computers to run more than one program at once (multi-tasking) and by the building of a very simple "cut and paste" macro, the drawback of not dictating directly to the application is minimised. Certainly, the greater accuracy of voice recognition more than counterbalances the necessity to cut and paste, and add-on programmes (not written by IBM) just coming to the market completely overcome this problem.

The overwhelming advantage of the IBM system is that corrections can be made at any time, indeed IBM recommend that a user does not look at the screen while dictating, allowing unbroken thought and, within the limitation only of discreet speech (see later), to continue to dictate as he has done in the past. Once text has been dictated the user makes any corrections and does not need to read the document again after printing (e.g. when signing).

All of the current systems have similar training requirements which take no longer than two hours. The user dictates a number of set sentences and, by this means, the computer learns how the individual user pronounces the 40 or so phonemes which together make up all of the sounds in the English language. It matters little whether the user has a broad Scottish accent or is a Cockney, what is required is that the computer learns how the user pronounces the relevant phonemes.

All current systems require "discreet speech". This is a piece of computer jargon which basically means that there must be a slight pause between each word dictated to enable the computer to understand where one word ends and another starts. Having isolated an individual word the computer then breaks the sounds of the word into groups of phonemes which it then compares with the dictionary of words stored as phonemes in its memory. The computer then will show on screen its first choice and then offer second, third, and fourth choices etc. in a list available for immediate correction. The IBM system holds the dictated word live while making a contextual grammar check as it may change its choice of words automatically.

After installation of these large and complex programs the first and major problem confronting any user is to learn to speak in the requisite "discreet speech." It sounds simple enough; the user must make a slight pause between words. In practice, however, a user will not pause between words but will either pause between syllables or, despite knowing that he must have a pause between each word, will still slur short words into each other.

To illustrate the problem, in ordinary speech one would slur the two words "fish shop" into one word with only one "sh" sound dragged from one word into the next so that it sounds like "fishop" with the "sh" element slightly elongated. The human brain has no difficulty in understanding the two words even though they have been slurred into each other. Here, the computer cannot compete with the human brain and hearing only one "sh" sound would be looking for - and not finding - a word spelt "fishop". The computer would then incorrectly guess at the word intended. The slight pause between each word when dictating in "discreet speech" means that the "sh" sound in "fish" and the "sh" sound in "shop" would both be pronounced, thereby permitting accurate interpretation.

It takes the average user a considerable time to learn to speak properly in discreet speech but speeds of anywhere between 65 and 90 words per minute are eventually possible.

The period of initial training for the three systems is two hours at most and is usually sufficient to enable the user to start working with the system immediately. The user must then be prepared to persevere, work with the system and correct errors so that the systems can learn how the user speaks and adapt to that method. An initial period of frustration and a feeling that productivity is slowed down is inevitable but the more the user operates the system the quicker that initial learning hump will be overcome.

It should not, for one moment, be thought that the use of voice recognition is limited to pure dictation. The computer can also work at command level (i.e. giving instructions to computer programs to take steps) but the real key to the use of the system is that, after some initial training in the creation of macros, the limit to the computer's use is the limit only of the user's imagination.

It is possible by giving two examples, one for *dictation macros* and the other for *command macros*, to illustrate how with a little thought and imagination voice recognition systems can and do become something a great deal more than simply a tool to input dictation and produce letters/documents from a word processor.

Dictation macro

To look firstly at a dictation macro it is necessary to understand that, while all systems come with adequate dictionaries of words, it is possible to add the user's own words. These of course can be words peculiar to the business of that user but the use of the imagination reveals that the computer will accept as accurate anything that it is told. If the user makes up his own word that is not in the dictionary and adds it to the dictionary then the computer will accept that made up word as being a real word for use. For example, if the user were to create a new word called "landlord-insure" and then instruct the computer that the new word means a series of key strokes which equate to the user's standard landlord insurance clause for a lease, the computer would accept that word and each time in drafting a lease when the user dictated "landlord-insure" the computer would put on the screen the user's precedent for that clause. It requires very little imagination from that point on to understand that it is possible to build letters or documents simply by the user utilising words that he has created for himself, as the new words can represent paragraphs of text.

A macro is simply a list of instructions to the computer which are grouped together and saved as a single name. That name can be activated by saying the one word. In the example above the macro was called with the one word "landlord-insure" and consisted of the key strokes necessary to reproduce the precedent for the landlord's insurance covenant - a dictation macro.

Command macro

A command macro is simply a series of commands executed one after another when the macro name is said. To illustrate, the steps required in most word processors to print a document are firstly from the menu bar on the screen to click, using the mouse, on "file." Thereafter from the drop-down menu that will appear to click on "print." Then a box appears in which the user must fill in the number of copies required and then click on the "OK" button. To print one copy therefore takes a series of steps. Using a voice command macro it is possible to create a word which when said will undertake one after the other the series of commands necessary. Accordingly, the steps that have been mentioned could be grouped together under a single word called "print-one." The marvellous element to the execution of command level macros is that the computer goes from one step to the next at the speed of the computer, while a user following the same steps himself could not go from one command to the next anywhere near as quickly.

The stage of command level macros at present is that more and more computer development companies are coming to realise that, by developing simple macros which describe the task required, it is possible for a person who knows nothing about the operation of a computer or of a word processor simply to say words appropriate for the task required, e.g. "print-one", and

the computer then undertakes that task creating at last the truly friendly computer.

Impact on the office

The introduction of the computer driven by voice onto the fee-earner's desk so that he becomes the point of production and produces his own letters, briefs, correspondence, etc. has considerable effects on the organisation and running of the office and a fundamental change in organisation becomes inevitable. It is not enough that the solicitor has the computer on his desk but as he becomes the point of production he must also have a printer and if he has a printer he must have supplies of letterheads, continuation paper, paper for file copies, envelopes and other stationery that surrounds the present day secretary.

Once the fee-earner has rearranged his office to conveniently accommodate all of these items he then has to consider the question of the location of his files: are they stored conveniently for his use or conveniently for access to the secretary? Who gets out the files with the post each day? Who puts copies on the files and, while mentioning copies, where in the office is the photocopier? Is it located conveniently for the typing pool or is it convenient to the fee-earner?

Many of these problems can now be overcome by the acquisition at approximately £1,000 of a single box, no bigger than the standard desk top computer, which incorporates a scanner, a fax modem, a copier and a printer. The fax modem will become of increasing importance as the fee-earner realises that with an appropriately worded macro he can say "fax-it" so that the document that he has dictated on screen will go immediately from his computer down the fax line. A scanner in the office is also likely to be necessary as the number of typing staff are reduced simply as being superfluous to requirements. In those circumstances a scanner which will accurately bring in a draft as if it had been typed becomes a necessity.

When used properly, voice recognition means that the writer can undertake his work immediately and when convenient to him and not just when the secretaries are in the office. There is no backlog of typing and files are always available to him instead of being in a queue waiting for the typist, and, as such, are available immediately to answer any telephone queries if necessary.

Without exception, every solicitor in the future must have increasing regard to costs and overheads. All are aware of the very low costs payable under the legal aid scheme and likely to be payable under the franchise. The reduction in overheads that voice recognition offers are likely to contribute greatly to the fee-earner being able to work successfully within those cost strictures and, as importantly, enable him to work quickly, at a convenient time with files always available.

Dragon, IBM and Phillips are now busy working on the next stage of computer voice recognition which will be the ability to speak to a computer in ordinary continuous speech. Indeed, Phillips claim to have such a system available for demonstration but at the time of going to press they do not have a system on the market that has been tried and tested for solicitors. The question that must be asked, whenever their product does eventually come to the market, is what will be its cost and how quickly can that cost bottom line? Prospective purchasers should enquire at the relevant time.

As upgraded systems are now clearly on the drawing board for all of the suppliers, it is sensible to ask whether or not one should wait for those superior systems to arrive. This must be a matter of individual choice but there are always developments in the computer market; if one does not make a decision to purchase at a given time but waits for the next round of improvements, one could wait forever. There are systems available now which can be on a fee-earner's desk immediately at a total cost of less than £3,000 and which ought to pay for themselves within four to six months and certainly prior to the upgrades coming onto the market.

Of equal importance is that by the time those improvements to the systems come on the market the user who is using voice recognition technology will have already made the fundamental changes in the way in which he has to work and in the reorganisation and logistics of his office. The quicker and the earlier the fundamental changes in office organisation are put in hand, then the easier it will be to absorb the upgrades of the future.

Voice recognition will be an integral part of the office of the future, but a word of warning to any partner wishing to purchase the system for members of his staff. Those staff members must firstly have a rudimentary knowledge of the office word processor but, more importantly, must be willing to adapt to the new systems. It is impossible to impose this type of technology on unwilling users as they will not put the necessary work into overcoming the hump of firstly learning to use the system and secondly working sufficiently with the system to allow it to learn how the individual user works and uses words.

Caution

Prospective purchasers should be wary of demonstrations where dictation is given at great speed to computers and then accurately reproduced. Salespeople tend to have a number of documents and "dictation macros" prepared that look immensely impressive but which are little more than a few conjurer's tricks. In the world of computers a little knowledge goes a long way! The reader should ask for a demonstration of all of the systems available but should always be armed with some standard documents or letters of their own and ask the demonstrator to dictate those documents to the system.

Traditionally conservative solicitors should have no fear of the coming of this new technology. A few hours invested in listening will overcome in-built prejudice against rapid computer advances. Computer voice recognition works, albeit with limitations, but those limitations can be overcome and the market place will dictate the survival only of those who can keep their costs in check. Partners should not leap at the first impressive demonstration but look at all the products available and see dealer's and manufacturer's demonstrations, read relevant sections of the appropriate magazines and newspapers and attend lectures but, above all, invest a little time, gain a little information and do what clients pay them to do - THINK!

Michael Kaye *is a solicitor and partner of Kaye Tesler solicitors.*

Company Profiles

ACCESS LEGAL SYSTEMS

Head Office: Station House, Station Road, Sandbach, Cheshire CW11 9JG

Tel: 01270 766774
Fax: 01270 766701
Helpdesk available
Normal office hours

Contact: G.E. Fowler, Director

Business established in 1980
No. of Directors 2
No. of Staff: 16
Target firm size: Any/All

PRODUCT DETAILS
Access Legal Accounting & Time Recording Systems

Environments Supported
Character-Based Terminal Emulation
DOS
Novell
Windows 3.x - CBT Emulation
Windows 3.x - Native
Windows 95 - 16 bit
Windows 95 - 32 bit
Windows NT

Application
Accounting - Accounts & Time Recording
Accounting - Accounts (no Time Recording)
Case Management - General Purpose
Legal Aid Franchising
Office Systems - Database - Clients and Contacts

Company Profile

ACCESS Legal Systems specialises in the legal marketplace with more than 350 lawyers' offices using its software for their accounting. These offices are located throughout England and Wales with installations as far apart as the West Country and the Northumbrian coast and with significant user presence in the cities of London, Manchester, Birmingham and Liverpool. The company also supplies systems outside the UK for subsidiaries of UK based practices and has a well established client base in Hong Kong, Dubai, Oman and Europe. The philosophy of the company has been to develop functional, reliable, user friendly applications and to provide full implementation, training, and support services for those applications. From the first installation users have been able to grow and migrate their applications to the latest technology platform without the need to change their data making the company one of the first in this market to support an "open" systems approach. The company products are available under the MS DOS, Windows and Novell Networking operating environment. The future aim of the company is to remain abreast of the changes taking place in the computer hardware and software marketplace and to make sure its users gain maximum cost benefit from the implementation of information technology. This is reflected in its most recent implementation of a client/server based Client Matter Database.

ACCOLADE SYSTEMS

Head Office: 12 Woodrow Court, Heybourne Road, London N17 0SX

Tel: 0181 365 0636
Fax: 0181 423 8855

Contact: Bryn Taylor, Consultant

Company Profile

Accolade Systems is an authorised re-seller of Timeslips, a highly cost-effective package for time and expense recording. Timeslips has over 100, 000 users world-wide and is used by solicitors and barristers in the UK and Europe. Prices start from £99 for a sole practitioner, £599 for a network in DOS or Windows and £300 for the AppleMac. The latest UK release includes: flat fees, fee notes, fees ledger, client funds, management reports, analysis of work-in-progress and profitability by client and fee-earner. Timeslips can be linked to other systems for remote data capture and additional analysis. Accolade systems provides consultancy services, demonstrations, implementation, training and support.

ACCULAW LTD

Head Office: 13 St Marks Road, Leamington Spa, Warwickshire CV32 6DL

Tel: 01926 886808
Helpdesk available
All hours

Contact: Tom Hervey, Managing Director

Business established in 1987
No. of Directors 2
No. of Staff: 2

PRODUCT DETAILS
Accudebt

Environments Supported
Windows 3.x - Native
Windows 95 - 16 bit

Application
Case Management - Debt Collection
Case Management - Mortgage Repossessions
Case Management - Uninsured Loss Recovery

Company Profile

Acculaw are specialist suppliers of debt collection and related systems. The company was started in 1987 by a solicitor with extensive debt collection experience and a passion for achieving legal and computational accuracy with minimum drudgery and maximum flexibility and ease of use. The company has always directed itself to the quality end of the market and has installed systems at some of the nation's leading law firms, including each of the "Big Four" firms in Birmingham. Careful attention to running costs has made Acculaw one of the most profitable and financially sound suppliers in the marketplace. Careful attention to serving its existing customers has ensured their continuing loyalty to (and indeed enthusiasm for) Accudebt, even the versions of the system running on Acorn ("BBC") hardware. With the latest version of the system running in Microsoft products under Windows on industry standard hardware, the company is ready to continue its successes into the next millenium.

ACE APPLIED COMPUTER EXPERTISE LIMITED

Head Office: 55-57 High Holborn, London WC1V 6DX

Tel: 0171 404 5577
Fax: 0171 404 5656
Helpdesk available
8.30am - 6.30pm

Contact: Stephen Murphy

Target firm size: Any / All

PRODUCT DETAILS
Cllix

Environments Supported
DOS
UNIX
Windows NT

Application
Electronic Publishing - Online Information Services

Felix

Environments Supported
DOS
UNIX
Windows NT

Application
Other

Infinity

Environments Supported
DOS
UNIX
Windows NT

Application
Accounting - Accounts (no Time Recording)
Case Management - General Purpose
Information Management - Document Management
Office Systems - Database - Marketing and Mailing
Office Systems - E-mail and shared Diary

Lix

Environments Supported
DOS
UNIX
Windows NT

Company Profile

ACE is the main system supplier to the Bar with over 80% of barristers using Infinity products. ACE also has a large solicitor client base. In April 1996 ACE took a major shareholding in LIX and the operation of the two companies merged adding LIX's products to ACE's portfolio. Infinity is ACE's Practice Management System which encompasses accounts, a practice-wide diary, case and document management, marketing database and management reporting. Built around a relational database, Infinity is the definitive Practice Management System. Cllix is an electronic court listing service which distributes the court listings daily to your PC. Felix is a user friendly group messaging system currently in use by High Court Judges.

ADROIT SOFTWARE LTD

Head Office: Unit 23, Grove Park, White Waltham, Maidenhead, Berkshire SL6 3LW

Tel: 01628 826568
Fax: 01628 826534

Contact: Chris Edwards, Technical Director

PRODUCT DETAILS
Case Manager

Environments Supported
Character-Based Terminal Emulation
UNIX
Windows 3.x - CBT Emulation

Application
Case Management - General Purpose
Case Management - Personal Injury

DocuManager

Environments Supported
Character-Based Terminal Emulation
UNIX
Windows 3.x - CBT Emulation

Application
Document Assembly Systems - General Purpose
Information Management - Document Management
Litigation Support - Document Listing Software

Company Profile
Established in 1980, Adroit Software provide high quality software solutions for the legal profession. Adroit Software's products include CaseManager, a flexible and powerful case management system, and DocuManager, the system for controlling documents in a multi-user word processing environment. The company is committed to Open Systems and offers its expertise in client/server, UNIX and PC systems to all through consultancy, bespoke software and training. Adroit Software specialises in rapid development of complete bespoke systems and amendments to third party software, using the Delphi code generators with most databases and office automation products.

AIM LAW DATA LTD

Head Office: 1 Royds Hall Road, Pavilion Business Park, Leeds, West Yorkshire LS12 6AJ

Tel: 0113 237 8500
Fax: 0113 263 1128
E-Mail: aim.leeds@dial.pipex.com

Contact: Rebecca Holt, Marketing Assistant
Contact: Stephen Taylor-Parker, Managing Director

PRODUCT DETAILS
Computer Telephony Integration

Debtco Progression

Document Image Processing

Progression

Company Profile
AIM Law Data's involvement in legal software dates from the early 1970s, and the creation of the first computerised debt recovery system - Debtco. Debtco 2 launched in the early 1980s is still the market leader in this specialist field, with over 200 installations. More recently AIM Law Data has developed CASMAN, a workflow management tool linked to Time Recording, which has rapidly assumed a dominant position, particularly with banks, building societies and Local Government legal departments. The success of Debtco 2 and CASMAN was combined at the beginning of 1996 with the launch of DEBTCO PROGRESSION - the new generation of arrears management software. With a Graphical User Interface screen presentation in Windows format, user-definable flowpath mapping allowing auto processing of complex conditions, MS-Office computability, superb escalation management capability and integrated links to telephony and document imaging technology, DEBTCO PROGRESSION has proved to be very user-friendly and functional.

A

AIM PROFESSIONAL

Head Office: Victoria House, 36 Derringham Street, Hull, North Humberside HU3 1EL

Tel: 01482 326971
Fax: 01482 228465
Helpdesk available

Contact: Jo Hunter, Marketeer

No. of Directors 3
No. of Staff: 8

Company Profile

AIM Professional has been supplying IT solutions to the legal profession for more than 20 years. AIM Evolution is the latest product on offer for the busy law firm of the 1990s. Universally acclaimed for its innovation and functionality, AIM Evolution uniquely provides a practice management system with core relational database and fully integrated workflow/case managment. AIM Evolution Workflow's flexibilty is particularly outstanding providing off-the-shelf procedures, yet allowing individual practice-specific developments. AIM Evolution features include the fee earner "Lawdesk" using Windows 3.11 or Windows 95, high levels of functionality, remarkable ease of use, on-screen billing and time recording and a powerful marketing module. Some of the ready made workflow procedures on offer are: residential conveyancing, re-mortgage conveyancing, criminal litigation, personal injury (RTA), matrimonial, debt recovery and basic trusts.

ALLVOICE COMPUTING PLC

Head Office: 20 Courtenay Park, Newton Abbot, Devon TQ12 2HB

Tel: 01626 331133
Fax: 01626 331150
E-Mail: 100257.760@compuserve.com

Contact: Don Bissell, Customer Services Manager

PRODUCT DETAILS
AllVoice Wordpress, IBM VoiceType, DragonDictate

Environments Supported
Windows 3.x - Native
Windows 95 - 16 bit

Application
Office Systems - Voice Recognition Systems

Company Profile

Established in 1980, AllVoice is Britain's leading independent supplier of voice recognition systems and is currently the only IBM BESTeam member for voice recognition in the UK, with offices in London as well as Head Office. In addition to the basic systems offered by IBM and Dragon, AllVoice has developed the world-beating WordExpress software allowing sole practitioners to produce their own letters and submissions without the need to learn computer or typing skills. Partners in larger firms can draft documents for later production or delegated correction by an assistant for quicker client response without incurring additional secretarial costs as well as completing their own work to a high standard at short notice or out of office hours. WordExpress is available for legal practices using Microsoft Word, WordPerfect and Lotus WordPro on both desktop and laptop computers and is supplied and supported by AllVoice direct and through a national network of authorised dealers.

"Only by seeing systems in action, can the potential of IT be fully assessed."

AXXIA SYSTEMS LTD

Head Office: 9 The Pavilions, Ruscombe Business Park, Twyford, Berkshire RG10 9NN

Tel: 01734 602602
Fax: 01734 602600
Helpdesk available
8.45am - 8.00pm

Contact: Caroline Franks
Contact: Doug Mclachlan, Development and Marketing Manager

Business established in 1995
No. of Directors 4
No. of Staff: 53
Target firm size: Medium, Large

PRODUCT DETAILS
Arista

Environments Supported
Character-Based Terminal Emulation
Windows 3.x - Native

Application
Accounting - Accounts & Time Recording
Case Management - Civil Litigation
Case Management - Conveyancing
Case Management - Criminal
Case Management - Debt Collection
Case Management - General Purpose
Case Management - Matrimonial
Case Management - Personal Injury
Case Management - Probate
Case Management - Road Traffic Act Claims
Case Management - Uninsured Loss Recovery
Information Management - Document Management
Information Management - Know-How
Office Systems - Database - Clients and Contacts
Office Systems - Database - Marketing and Mailing
Office Systems - Desk-top Faxing
Office Systems - E-mail and shared Diary
Office Systems - Fee Earner Desktop

Company Profile

When you buy a new computer system, you are beginning a relationship with your supplier which needs to last at least as long as the system itself. What's more, you need to make sure that your supplier can keep pace with the rapid changes in information technology that experience shows are continuous. Axxia has a tradition of service to the legal profession stretching back to 1968, when Kienzle Data Systems first supplied systems for solicitors. Axxia offers you innovation with tradition, dynamism with peace of mind. Axxia is the largest supplier totally dedicated to the legal market. Axxia can supply complete front and back office systems or can supply departmental fee-earner support systems for specific functions like conveyancing or personal injury. Many of Axxia's customers have been using systems from Axxia Systems and its predecessors through several generations of development. With the support of an active independent user group, Axxia is committed to maintain its market-leading position as a supplier of systems for solicitors. The company has a policy of continual enhancement of its products and services.

C-LAW SOLICITORS SYSTEMS

Head Office: 113B Fore Street, Kingsbridge, South Devon TQ7 1BG

Tel: 01548 857775
Fax: 01548 857775
E-Mail: rossetti@c-law.zynet.co.uk
Helpdesk available
9.00am - 5.30pm

Contact: Geoffrey Rossetti, System Designer

Business established in 1987
No. of Directors 1
No. of Staff: 1
Target firm size: Small, Medium

PRODUCT DETAILS
C-Law Accounts & Time Recording

Environments Supported
DOS
Windows 3.x - Native
Windows 95 - 16 bit

Application
Accounting - Accounts & Time Recording
Accounting - Accounts (no Time Recording)

Company Profile
Accounting and/or Integrated Time Recording system for the small to medium sized firms (1 - 15 fee earners). System produced by a practising Solicitor and being continually enhanced and updated. Has been supplied in its various forms to firms since 1985 mainly personal recommendation. Users comment favourably on how easy they find it to operate and understand. This means that minimal staff training is needed. The package includes all standard accounting & time recording and costing functions, deposit interest calculations, monthly reports & analyses, expense projections. It can be supplied for accounting only functions if required at a reduced price. Needs IBM or compatible PC and dot matrix, inkjet or laser printer. The system is DOS based and has a minimal hardware requirement, but the set-up procedure is capable of creating a new Windows program group and program icon within the Windows desktop for users who require to operate the system via Windows. Comes with instruction manual and installation disk for user installation. If users require will be installed and set up for them on site. A demonstration disk is available. Experience shows that minimal support is needed, but contract is available.

CMS OPEN

Head Office: 11-13 Capricorn Centre, Cranes Farm Road, Basildon, Essex SS14 3JJ

Tel: 01268 270601
Fax: 01268 270602
E-Mail: cms@quintec.co.uk
Helpdesk available
Normal office hours

Contact: Michael Bailey, Business Manager

Business established in 1991
No. of Directors 4
No. of Staff: 40
Target firm size: Any/All

PRODUCT DETAILS
CMS Open

Environments Supported
Windows 3.x - Native
Windows 95 - 16 bit
Windows 95 - 32 bit
Windows NT

Application
Accounting - Accounts & Time Recording
Office Systems - Database - Clients and Contacts
Office Systems - Database - Marketing and Mailing
Office Systems - Fee Earner Desktop

Company Profile
Part of QUINTEC INTERNATIONAL

COGNITO SOFTWARE LTD

Head Office: Flair House, 130 High Street, Crediton, Devon EX17 3LQ

Tel: 01363 775582
Fax: 01363 773952
Helpdesk available
9.00am - 5.30pm

Contact: Shirley Turner, Marketing Administrator

Business established in 1991
No. of Directors 2
No. of Staff: 15
Target firm size: Any / All

PRODUCT DETAILS
Cognito

Environments Supported
DOS
Novell
Windows 3.x - Native
Windows 95 - 16 bit
Windows 95 - 32 bit

Application
Accounting - Accounts & Time Recording
Information Management - Document Management
Legal Aid Franchising
Office Systems - Database - Clients and Contacts
Office Systems - Fee Earner Desktop

Custodiens

Environments Supported
DOS
Novell
Windows 95 - 16 bit
Windows 95 - 32 bit

Application
Accounting - Estate Accounts
Accounting - Trust Accounts

Company Profile
Cognito Software products may be purchased through our network of specialist legal centres based in Birmingham, Newcastle, Manchester, Leeds, West London and Exeter. This ensures we provide a knowledgeable yet local service. The Cognito "BACK OFFICE" Accounts and Administration package links to the market-leading case management product DPS.

CONTEXT LIMITED

Head Office: Grand Union House, 20 Kentish Town Road, London NW1 9NR

Tel: 0171 267 8989
Fax: 0171 267 1133
E-Mail: sales@context.co.uk
Helpdesk available
9.30am - 5.30pm

Contact: Michelle Green, Marketing Director

Business established in 1986
No. of Directors 4
No. of Staff: 30
Target firm size: Any / All

PRODUCT DETAILS
Electronic Publishing/Cd-Roms

Environments Supported
DOS
Windows 3.x - Native

Application
Electronic Publishing - Online Information Services
Electronic Publishing - Other

Company Profile
Context Limited is an independent electronic publisher specialising in business and professional areas. Founded in 1986, Context has secured a leading position in this sector, concentrating particularly on United Kingdom and European Community law and official information. Adding value to comprehensive, authoritative information archives is Context's strength. Context obtains data in a variety of formats from many sources. Information is restructured, enhanced and consolidated then published with advanced search software on the most appropriate electronic media including CD-ROM and online. Users of our titles benefit from a straightforward user interface that incorporates full-text searching with an ever increasing set of sophisticated features. Our products are backed up by professionals who understand the data and can explain how to use the products to the best advantage. Context publishes the JUSTIS range of database products and is developing a new range of business information services starting with Context Tenders. The JUSTIS range includes UK and European legislation, case law and other official information. Titles include JUSTIS Weekly Law Reports, Jordans Family Law Reports, Statutory Instruments and the Electronic Law Reports with over 130 years of case reporting.

C

CPL LIMITED

Head Office: Liverpool House, Penlan Street, Pwllheli, Gwynedd LL53 5DE

Tel: 01758 613035
Fax: 01758 612485
Helpdesk available
9.00am - 5.00pm

Contact: Susannah Robinson, Customer Support Manager

Business established in 1980
No. of Directors 2
No. of Staff: 8
Target firm size: Small, Medium

PRODUCT DETAILS
Accounts 2 for the Solicitor

Environments Supported
DOS

Application
Accounting - Accounts & Time Recording
Accounting - Accounts (no Time Recording)
Case Management - General Purpose
Legal Aid Franchising
Office Systems - Database - Clients and Contacts

Company Profile
CPL Ltd was established in 1980 and has a proven track record in the legal field having supplied accounting software for solicitors since 1984. "Accounts 2 for the Solicitor", in use in practices throughout England and Wales, is constantly revised in response to user feed back and changes in Law Society requirements. The standard package can be tailored to individual needs. All work is carried out to BS5750 guidelines. "Accounts 2 for the Solicitor" is specifically designed for the small to medium sized practice. Years of close liaison with the target market has led to CPL's enviable knowledge of the needs of today's busy practice.

CURAT LEX LIMITED

Head Office: 12 St Peter's Churchyard, Derby DE1 1TZ

Tel: 01332 298979
Fax: 01332 347552
E-Mail: clex@link.org
Helpdesk available
9.00am - 5.00pm

Contact: Charles Daborn, Business Development Manager
Contact: John Waldron, Director

Business established in 1991
No. of Directors 2
No. of Staff: 4
Target firm size: Small to Medium/Large

PRODUCT DETAILS
Sovereign LAW

Environments Supported
DOS
Novell
UNIX
Windows 3.x - Native
Windows 95 - 16 bit
Windows 95 - 32 bit
Windows NT

Application
Accounting - Accounts & Time Recording
Case Management - General Purpose
Legal Aid Franchising
Office Systems - Database - Clients and Contacts
Office Systems - Database - Marketing and Mailing
Office Systems - Fee Earner Desktop

Sovereign Professional

Environments Supported
DOS
Novell
UNIX
Windows 3.x - Native
Windows 95 - 16 bit
Windows 95 - 32 bit
Windows NT

Application
Accounting - Accounts & Time Recording
Case Management - General Purpose
Office Systems - Database - Clients and Contacts
Office Systems - Database - Marketing and Mailing

Company Profile

Curat Lex is a specialist software house dedicated to the development and support of affordable and effective integrated front and back office accounting and practice management systems designed by solicitors for solicitors using industry standard development tools from Sage and Microsoft. The software benefits from access to the Sage Sovereign ODBC driver for connectivity with Microsoft Office products, the Windows Report Writer and components from Sovereign for Windows. Sovereign Professional is newly released and offers Client/Contact Database, Office & Client Accounting, Time Recording and Reporting running in conjunction with Sage Sovereign. Sovereign LAW is the complete Practice Management system containing all the features of Professional plus Fee-earner support, Quality Control, Legal Aid Franchising and Case Management and is eminently suited to networking. The software is multi-platform compatible and runs on inter alia NetWare 4.1, Windows NT and Windows 95. Curat Lex has particular experience of installation on pure Windows 95 networks. The design, set up, installation and training for Sovereign LAW Case Management is charged as a service at an agreed rate depending on the amount of work involved in configuring available examples to the users' precise requirements.

DART REFLEX GROUP

Head Office: Wyboston Lakes Business Village, Great North Road, Wyboston, Bedfordshire MK44 3AL

Tel: 01480 470307
Fax: 01480 218033
Helpdesk available
Normal office hours

Contact: Geoff Morris, Director
Contact: Tim Carter, Sales Manager

Business established in 1993
No. of Directors 4
No. of Staff: 20
Target firm size: Medium, Large

PRODUCT DETAILS
PPL - Productivity Practice-wide for Lawyers

Environments Supported
Novell
UNIX
Windows 3.x - Native
Windows 95 - 32 bit
Windows NT

Application
Accounting - Accounts & Time Recording
Case Management - Civil Litigation
Case Management - Conveyancing
Case Management - Criminal
Case Management - Debt Collection
Case Management - General Purpose
Case Management - Landlord & Tenant
Case Management - Probate
Document Assembly Systems - General Purpose
Document Assembly Systems - Letter Writing
Information Management - Document Management
Information Management - Know-How
Information Management - Text Retrieval Software
Legal Aid Franchising
Litigation Support - Document Listing Software
Litigation Support - Image-based Discovery Systems
Office Systems - Database - Clients and Contacts
Office Systems - Database - Marketing and Mailing
Office Systems - Desk-top Faxing
Office Systems - E-mail and shared Diary
Office Systems - Fee Earner Desktop
Office Systems - Scanning Imaging and OCR
Office Systems - Voice Recognition Systems
Other

Company Profile

Dart Legal Systems was created in 1993 to distribute an Australian practice management system developed by the Managing Partner of a 150-strong law firm. In 1995, Dart acquired full development and support rights to this product, and set up with a well-established systems house, Reflex, a joint venture company, the Dart-Reflex Group, to market, support and develop the product within the UK, all to ISO 9001 accreditation. The outcome of this merger was a new product, PPL (Productivity Practice-wide for Lawyers). PPL is a fully Windows-compliant product, and will operate across UNIX, Novell or NT networks. Created and developed using one of the most powerful nested relational database systems world-wide (Unidata), PPL presents a practice-wide database platform for all transactions, whether financial or not, to be entered via its unique "FeeBook". Combining commercial style accounting and time recording with flexible case management and intelligent document wide production facilities, the user is presented with a ready-made system, or can have available a wide range of tailorable options, to ensure that the solution fits the firm, and not the other way round. In conjunction with Fisher Meredith, a wide range of additional facilities have been incorporated into the product, to assist in the profitability of all firms operating a Legal Aid Franchise. These include Clawback, Bill of Costs in Taxable Form and a wide range of completely integrated legal aid billing routes, linking into Laserforms forms. Dart's integration facilities have been further enhanced following their association with Barratt Edwards International (BEI), who are Novell's top integrator and supporter of SoftSolutions and Groupwise products.

DP ADVISERS LIMITED

Head Office: Glen House, Stag Place, London SW1E 5AG

Tel: 0171 834 4068
Fax: 0171 630 7952

Contact: Kelvin McGregor Alcorn, Director

PRODUCT DETAILS

Application

Information Management - Document Management
Litigation Support - Image-based Discovery Systems
Office Systems - Scanning Imaging and OCR

Company Profile

Established in 1967, and specialising in Electronic Document Management since 1990, DP Advisers provides EGAMI-LEGAL software, consultancy, and services to support litigation, know-how and document management to its extensive UK and international client base. Documents are image-scanned, stored, and linked to user definable index cards for capturing key or relevant information. Searches will display both the index card and document image. Full text retrieval is provided with OCR and "fuzzy searching". DP Advisers offers the full range of document management services - consultancy, database design, document scanning/coding, rekeying - which can be performed at a client or DP Advisers' facility.

"Integration is at the heart of new office technology. A good integrated package means that the user does not have to know which piece of software is doing which particular task."

ECLIPSE LEGAL SYSTEMS

Head Office: Merchants House, Peckover Street, Little Germany, Bradford BD1 5BD

Tel: 01274 395299
Fax: 01274 733409
Helpdesk available
9.00am - 5.30pm

Contact: Russell Thomson, Sales Director

Business established in 1977
No. of Directors 2
No. of Staff: 10

PRODUCT DETAILS
Chase II Chase IV Windows

Environments Supported
Character-Based Terminal Emulation
DOS
Novell
UNIX
Windows 3.x - CBT Emulation
Windows 3.x - Native
Windows 95 - 16 bit
Windows 95 - 32 bit
Windows NT

Application
Accounting - Accounts & Time Recording
Case Management - Civil Litigation
Case Management - Conveyancing
Case Management - Criminal
Case Management - Debt Collection
Case Management - General Purpose
Case Management - Personal Injury
Case Management - Probate
Case Management - Road Traffic Act Claims
Case Management - Uninsured Loss Recovery
Document Assembly Systems - General Purpose
Electronic Publishing - Legal Forms
Information Management - Document Management
Legal Aid Franchising
Office Systems - Database - Clients and Contacts
Office Systems - Database - Marketing and Mailing
Office Systems - Desk-top Faxing

Company Profile

Eclipse Legal Systems provides a specialist service to Solicitors in Private Practice, Commercial Companies and Multinationals. We provide a consultancy approach to system sales, installing systems which match clients' expectations. Our experience in systems integration allows us to link existing systems giving totally integrated seamless systems. At Eclipse we constantly update our software to reflect the feedback from our users and, uniquely, provide all of our users with the updated software. Chase Case Management can be installed with or without Chase Accounts, modules are available for Medical Negligence, Accidents at Work, Industrial Diseases and Road Traffic Accidents. Additional modules are available for Matrimonial, Housing, Conveyancing and Probate. As a systems house we are heavily resourced with programmers and support staff and are pleased to work closely with Consultants and other Law Society listed suppliers.

E

EDGEBYTE COMPUTERS LTD

Head Office: 5 Queens Square, Poulton-le-Fylde, Lancashire FY6 7BW

Tel: 01253 899311
Fax: 01253 899015
Helpdesk available
9.00am - 5.00pm

Contact: Nigel Bernstein, Sales Director

Business established in 1990
No. of Directors 3
No. of Staff: 5
Target firm size: Small, Medium

PRODUCT DETAILS
Lawbyte Conveyancing System

Environments Supported
DOS
Windows 3.x - CBT Emulation
Windows 3.x - Native
Windows 95 - 16 bit
Windows 95 - 32 bit
Windows NT

Application
Case Management - Conveyancing

Lawbyte Solicitors Accounts & Time Recording

Environments Supported
DOS
Windows 3.x - CBT Emulation
Windows 3.x - Native
Windows 95 - 16 bit
Windows 95 - 32 bit
Windows NT

Application
Accounting - Accounts & Time Recording
Legal Aid Franchising
Other

Lawbyte Solicitors Database

Environments Supported
DOS
Windows 3.x - CBT Emulation
Windows 3.x - Native
Windows 95 - 16 bit
Windows 95 - 32 bit
Windows NT

Application
Legal Aid Franchising
Miscellaneous - Other
Office Systems - Database - Clients and Contacts
Office Systems - Database - Marketing and Mailing
Office Systems - Desk-top Faxing
Office Systems - E-mail and shared Diary
Office Systems - Fee Earner Desktop

Company Profile
Edgebyte Computers Ltd specialises in software solutions for the legal profession. At Edgebyte we pride ourselves on the strength of our software products and the quality of the professional software support provided to our clients. Our Lawbyte system is a fully featured, comprehensive package covering all areas of Solicitors Accounts and Time Recording. The system has all the features normally found in a package costing many thousands of pounds including full financial accounting (office/client/deposit accounts), profit & loss, balance sheet, budgeting, bank reconciliation, interest calculation, debtor's letters, link to word processing. The system is designed to be menu driven and user friendly. The Lawbyte software package costs £995. Combined software/hardware packages are available from £1845. Additional licences for multi-user network workstations cost £295. The system runs on any compatible PC under DOS, Windows or network systems.

Information Technology Directory

If you would like to be included in the 1997 edition of the Law Society's Information Technology Directory please write

Debra Salvoni, The Law Society, 50-52 Chancery Lane, London WC2A 1SX, Fax: 0171 404 1124

THE LAW SOCIETY

E

ELEETIX SOFTWARE LTD

Head Office: 140 Tabernacle Street, London EC2A 4SD

Tel: 0171 251 5556
Fax: 0171 251 5557
Helpdesk available
9.00am - 5.30pm

Contact: Mark Gibbons, Director

Business established in 1990
No. of Directors 2
No. of Staff: 9

PRODUCT DETAILS
Probase Connect (PBC), PBC Litigation, PBC Probate, PBC Trust

Environments Supported
Macintosh System 7.x
Windows 3.x - Native
Windows 95 - 16 bit
Windows 95 - 32 bit
Windows NT

Application
Accounting - Accounts (no Time Recording)
Accounting - Estate Accounts
Case Management - Civil Litigation
Case Management - General Purpose
Case Management - Probate
Document Assembly Systems - General Purpose
Financial Services - General
Legal Aid Franchising
Litigation Support - Document Listing Software
Office Systems - Database - Clients and Contacts
Office Systems - Database - Marketing and Mailing
Office Systems - Fee Earner Desktop

EMOS INFORMATION SYSTEMS LTD

Head Office: EMOS House, 2 Treadway Technical Centre, Treadway Hill, High Wycombe, Buckinghamshire HP10 9Rs

Tel: 01628 850400
Fax: 01628 850251
Helpdesk available

Contact: David Rogers, Managing Director

Business established in 1983
No. of Directors 1
No. of Staff: 63
Target firm size: Any / All

PRODUCT DETAILS
Copitrak Family Systems

Environments Supported
DOS

Application
Accounting - Accounts (no Time Recording)
Calculators - Expense of Time
Information Management - Document Management
Miscellaneous - Other

Excelsior LawDesk Limited

Head Office: Summerfields, Furners Lane, Henfield, West Sussex BN5 9HS

Tel: 01273 494978
E-Mail: lawdesk@pavilion.co.uk

Contact: David Williams, Managing Director

Business established in 1995
No. of Directors 2
Target firm size: Any / All

Product Details
ProbateDesk

Environments Supported
Windows 3.x - Native
Windows 95 - 16 bit
Windows 95 - 32 bit

Application
Accounting - Estate Accounts
Case Management - Probate

Company Profile

The company has been recently established by a practising solicitor to market his own proposed range of specialist template products using generally available software. The first product launched is ProbateDesk, an estate accounts preparation tool based on the Microsoft Excel spreadsheet program. ProbateDesk also includes extensive checklists to assist with better management of probate matters. The company seeks to deliver a high level of personal attention well attuned to the needs of practising solicitors.

F & F Systems

Head Office: Cotswold House, Nympsfield, Gloucestershire GL10 3TY

Tel: 01453 860080
Fax: 01453 861005
Helpdesk available
9.00am - 5.30pm

Contact: Brian Pittaway

Business established in 1992
No. of Directors 2
No. of Staff: 5

Product Details
ICAS

Environments Supported
Character-Based Terminal Emulation
DOS
Novell
UNIX
Windows 3.x - Native
Windows NT

Application
Case Management - Civil Litigation
Case Management - Conveyancing
Case Management - Criminal
Case Management - Debt Collection
Case Management - General Purpose
Case Management - Landlord & Tenant
Case Management - Personal Injury
Case Management - Road Traffic Act Claims
Case Management - Uninsured Loss Recovery
Litigation Support - Document Listing Software
Office Systems - Database - Clients and Contacts

"As with most things in life, you get what you pay for. A good rule is to buy the best equipment you can afford, rather than the cheapest you can find."

Company Profile

F&F Systems, established in 1992, is a relative newcomer to the legal software market. Yet the directors and staff of the company have many years experience (over 38 years between them) working for other major suppliers in the legal field. The two directors have drawn on this great store of knowledge and expertise when developing the ICAS software and incorporated the features and requirements requested by clients over many years. The range of products includes case management, personal injury, debt recovery and litigation support. F&F Systems believes that it can offer all the advantages of a small company without the disadvantages by offering a personal service, close development links with clients, great personal commitment on the part of both the directors and all employees of the company, swift and efficient technical back-up and a prompt response to clients' needs and requirements. F&F Systems has an open policy on interfacing with legal accounts systems. ICAS is the Case Management System recommended by a major supplier of accounts systems and also encompasses a link with Laserforms. The company also offers a consultancy service and is currently working with some of the largest commercial organisations in the country.

INDEPENDENT SYSTEMS ASSOCIATES

Head Office: Grosvenor Court, Lea Hall Enterprise Park, Armitage Road, Rugeley, Staffordshire WS15 1LH

Tel: 01889 583 640
Fax: 01889 575 715
E-Mail: 100340, 1554compuserve
Helpdesk available
Normal office hours

Contact: Warwick Bourton, Sales Director

Business established in 1990
No. of Directors 2
No. of Staff: 20
Target firm size: Medium, Large

PRODUCT DETAILS
Specialised Bespoke Systems, Windows 95 Training

Environments Supported
Windows 3.x - Native
Windows 95 - 16 bit
Windows 95 - 32 bit
Windows NT

Application
Miscellaneous - Other

Company Profile

ISA is a software house specialising in project management and analysis. We make pragmatic use of the government standard PRINCE and SSADM methods. We are a Microsoft Solutions Provider and we develop Windows based client/server systems using Microsoft products. We have provided services and systems to a number of private companies and Government departments.

INFORMATION FOR LAWYERS LIMITED

Head Office: 509 Upper Richmond Road, London SW14 7EE

Tel: 0181 878 3033
Fax: 0181 876 8484
E-Mail: NickHolmes@infolaw.co.uk

Contact: Adam Blackstone, Product Manager
Contact: Nick Holmes, Director

Business established in 1991
No. of Directors 1
No. of Staff: 5

PRODUCT DETAILS
FT Law & Tax Precedents On Disk

Environments Supported
DOS
Macintosh System 7.x
UNIX
Windows 3.x - CBT Emulation
Windows 3.x - Native
Windows 95 - 16 bit
Windows 95 - 32 bit
Windows NT

Application
Electronic Publishing - Precedents

HotDocs (Document Assembly)

Environments Supported
DOS
Windows 3.x - CBT Emulation
Windows 3.x - Native
Windows 95 - 16 bit
Windows 95 - 32 bit
Windows NT

Application
Document Assembly Systems - General Purpose
Information Management - Document Management

QuickDivorce

Environments Supported
DOS
Windows 3.x - CBT Emulation
Windows 3.x - Native
Windows 95 - 16 bit
Windows 95 - 32 bit
Windows NT

Application
Case Management - Matrimonial

QuickWill (Document Assembly)

Environments Supported
DOS
Windows 3.x - CBT Emulation
Windows 3.x - Native
Windows 95 - 16 bit
Windows 95 - 32 bit
Windows NT

Application
Document Assembly Systems - Will Drafting

Company Profile

Information for Lawyers Limited is a specialist publisher aiming to meet the document production and information needs of practising lawyers. IFL publishes FT Law & Tax Precedents on Disk, the most widely-used and highly-regarded libraries of WP precedents for all commercial agreements, conveyances, leases, wills, trust deeds, county court and matrimonial work. IFL has also developed fully-automated document drafting (document assembly) systems, including the market-leading QuickWill and QuickDivorce for matrimonial petitions. New in 1996 is a range of electronic forms and workflow applications developed with the outstanding HotDocs technology. IFL also provides consultancy services for all aspects of database and CD-ROM production, document management and legal information. IFL is committed to the development of affordable off-the-shelf information applications of real use to the majority of practitioners, not just the "legal 500" and is always keen to hear from practitioners with clearly-expressed information needs or who have material for publication. IFL's Web site is at http://www.infolaw.co.uk/ifl.

INFORMATION HORIZONS LTD

Head Office: Athene House, 66-73 Shoe Lane, London EC4A 3BQ

Tel: 0171 353 6500
Fax: 0171 353 6501
Helpdesk available
Normal office hours

Contact: Andrew Beardwood

Business established in 1991
No. of Directors 2
No. of Staff: 8
Target firm size: Any / All

PRODUCT DETAILS
Market Edge

Environments Supported
DOS
Windows 3.x - Native
Windows 95 - 32 bit
Windows NT

Application
Office Systems - Database - Clients and Contacts
Office Systems - Database - Marketing and Mailing
Office Systems - Desk-top Faxing
Office Systems - E-mail and shared Diary
Office Systems - Fee Earner Desktop

Company Profile
Information Horizons is also a Microsoft Authorised Training Centre and provides training courses in Microsoft's range of desktop software packages.

INFORMATION PROVIDERS LIMITED

Head Office: DMR House, 8-10 Cleave Avenue, Farnborough, Kent BR6 7HB

Tel: 01689 860000
Fax: 01689 860330
E-Mail: ptc@ipl.co.uk
Helpdesk available
24 hours (Internet)

Contact: Paul Carpenter, Director

Business established in 1969
No. of Directors 3
No. of Staff: 18
Target firm size: Any / All

PRODUCT DETAILS
Application
Electronic Publishing - Legal Forms
Electronic Publishing - Online Information Services
Electronic Publishing - Other
Information Management - Document Management
Information Management - Library Systems
Information Management - Text Retrieval Software

Company Profile
Information Providers Limited is part of the DMR Information and Technology Group which includes DMR Computer Limited and CompuForms, the legal forms publisher. IPL can undertake and provide information systems both in-house and online for a wide variety of legal applications. Online systems incorporated within Web sites can be hosted on IPL's network of Internet servers. IPL's own Web site is at http://www.ipl.co.uk.

IT Accounting

Head Office: IT House, 37 Berry Head Road, Brixham, Devon TQ5 9AA

Tel: 01803 856566
Fax: 01803 856567
Helpdesk available
Normal office hours

Contact: Trevor Howarth
Contact: Richard White, Managing Partner

Business established in 1982
No. of Directors 3
No. of Staff: 8
Target firm size: Small, Medium

Product Details
IT Accounting

Environments Supported
DOS
Windows 3.x - Native

Application
Accounting - Accounts & Time Recording
Accounting - Accounts (no Time Recording)
Case Management - General Purpose
Legal Aid Franchising
Office Systems - Database - Clients and Contacts

Company Profile
Established in 1982, IT specialises in developing programs for Solicitors, Accountants and Architects. We'll supply a copy of our Cashier program with a full tutorial for you to try on your computer, against a refundable deposit of £20. You can enter some of your own data and have full access to every routine and report. The Tutorial takes you, key-by-key, through typical entries and producing reports. It is supported by an exhaustive Reference Manual with easy-to-use self-installation routines and instructions. Hot line telephone support starts for as little as £65 a year and includes free revisions, automatically, as often as we release them, ensuring that you are always using the very latest revision. IT Accounting publishes the "Idiot's Guide to Computing", a complimentary copy of which is available to practices interested in computerisation.

James Strachan & Co

Head Office: 117 Thetford Street, New Malden, Surrey KT3 5DS

Tel: 0181 336 2700
Fax: 0181 942 0307
E-Mail: compuserve 100560, 574
Helpdesk available
9.00am - 5.00pm

Contact: James Strachan, Proprietor

Business established in 1985
No. of Directors 1
No. of Staff: 2
Target firm size: Small

Product Details
Strongbox

Environments Supported
DOS
Windows 3.x - Native
Windows 95 - 16 bit

Application
Accounting - Accounts & Time Recording
Information Management - Document Management
Office Systems - Database - Clients and Contacts

Company Profile
Strongbox Accounting Systems have been in use since 1987 and have been installed in over 250 sites. Our products are designed for the small practice and we have made them as easy to use as possible. We do not restrict use to one machine per licence. Once you have purchased our product you may install it on as many machines as you wish under a single licence for no extra cost. A variety of software utilities are available to members of our maintenance scheme free of charge. Our annual charge for maintenance is currently £150.

J

JORDANS

Head Office: 21 St Thomas Street, Bristol, Avon BS1 6JS

Tel: 0117 923 0600
Fax: 0117 923 0063
Helpdesk available
9.00am - 5.00pm

Contact: Geoff Willcock, Director - Sales Customer Support

Business established in 1863
No. of Directors 7
No. of Staff: 240
Target firm size: Any / All

PRODUCT DETAILS
Customer Ordering On-Line (Cool)

Environments Supported
Character-Based Terminal Emulation

Application
Electronic Publishing - Legal Forms
Electronic Publishing - Online Information Services
Office Systems - Database - Marketing and Mailing

Financial Analysis Made Easy (Fame)

Environments Supported
DOS
Windows 3.x - CBT Emulation

Application
Electronic Publishing - Online Information Services
Office Systems - Database - Clients and Contacts

Forms On Disk

Environments Supported
DOS

Application
Electronic Publishing - Legal Forms

PC Secretary

Environments Supported
DOS

Application
Electronic Publishing - Legal Forms
Information Management - Document Management
Office Systems - Database - Clients and Contacts

Company Profile

Jordans Limited was founded in 1863, principally to register companies and to perform other administration tasks on behalf of professional and other customers. A comprehensive range of products and services now extends far beyond those core activities and caters for numerous other professional and corporate requirements. We are developing a range of software products to enhance the delivery of a growing number of our products and services. To enhance our UK company formation and administration services, we are now able to offer wide ranging overseas services from our growing International Department, in particular, Jordans act in the registration of offshore companies for International Trading and Asset Protection. Jordans is also a major provider of business information. Detailed financial information on public and private companies is available online through major hosts or direct. We provide the best-selling CD-ROM "Fame" and a series of mainland Europe CD products. We render a unique company information service and a full range of search facilities UK and worldwide. Our range also includes Company and Family Law publications.

JV Legal

Head Office: Blakedown House, Village Farm Estate, Pyle, Mid Glamorgan CF33 6NU

Tel: 01656 741413
Fax: 01656 745534

Contact: Martin Bowen, Sales Manager
Contact: Vernon Hopkins, Partner

No. of Directors 2
No. of Staff: 18
Target firm size: Any / All

Product Details
Cat 5 Cabling, DPS, Cognito, Custodiens, Novell, Printaform, IBM/AllVoice, WordPerfect, Word

Environments Supported
DOS
Windows 3.x - Native
Windows 95 - 32 bit

Application
Accounting - Accounts & Time Recording
Accounting - Accounts (no Time Recording)
Accounting - Estate Accounts
Accounting - Trust Accounts
Calculators - Child Support Act
Case Management - Civil Litigation
Case Management - Conveyancing
Case Management - Criminal
Case Management - Debt Collection
Case Management - General Purpose
Case Management - Personal Injury
Case Management - Probate
Case Management - Uninsured Loss Recovery
Document Assembly Systems - Will Drafting
Electronic Publishing - Legal Forms
Electronic Publishing - Online Information Services
Legal Aid Franchising
Office Systems - Database - Clients and Contacts
Office Systems - Desk-top Faxing
Office Systems - E-mail and shared Diary
Office Systems - Fee Earner Desktop

Company Profile
JV Legal - A one stop solution. Over 200 installed sites. ISO 9002 and BS5750 Registered Company. Part of JV Group which includes JV Telecoms (installation and maintenance of PABX systems) and JV Systems (hardware, software and maintenance of office equipment).

Keystone Systems UK Ltd

Head Office: 137 Aldersgate Street, London EC1A 4LL

Tel: 0171 600 7576
Fax: 0171 796 0796
Helpdesk available
Normal office hours

Contact: Colin Morris, General Manager
Contact: Kaye Sycamore, Marketing Manager

Business established in 1996
No. of Directors 3
No. of Staff: 5
Target firm size: Large

Product Details
Keystone Professional Practice Management

Environments Supported
Macintosh System 7.x
Novell
UNIX
Windows 3.x - Native
Windows NT

Application
Accounting - Accounts & Time Recording
Case Management - General Purpose
Office Systems - Database - Clients and Contacts
Office Systems - Database - Marketing and Mailing
Office Systems - Quality Management/Client Care Steps

Company Profile
Keystone is a fully integrated accounts and practice management system designed for use by fee-earners as well as central accounts. Written in Oracle and launched in the last quarter of 1995 it is in the process of being implemented (or evaluated) by several of the largest firms in New Zealand and Australia. The product is available in the UK from our subsidiary company Keystone Systems UK Limited. The first sale to a top ten firm in the UK was completed in March 1996. Keystone is fully graphical and supports multiple offices, multiple firms and multiple currencies.

KOLVOX

Head Office: 79 Knightsbridge, London SW1X 7RB

Tel: 0171 245 9312
Fax: 0171 235 2683

Contact: Tim Waggett, Sales Director

Business established in 1990
No. of Directors 2
No. of Staff: 5
Target firm size: Any / All

PRODUCT DETAILS
Kolvox LawTALK

Environments Supported
Windows 3.x - Native
Windows 95 - 32 bit

Application
Office Systems - Voice Recognition Systems

Company Profile

LawTALK for Windows is a productivity tool that allows professionals to use the full potential of their computers through speech input. LawTALK's intuitive voice commands for dictation, navigation, command and control, and formatting are easy to learn and use. LawTALK is much more than a basic speech recognition engine that allows you to talk to your computer. With LawTALK, you talk to your application at a task level, for faster learning, ease of use and improved productivity. The LawTALK user does not have to know how to type or how to use specific computer software. Instead of memorising unfamiliar keystrokes or working through a series of pull-down menus, the user can say simple commands such as "create letter", "underline paragraph" or "print document". Spoken commands can be intermixed with keyboard and mouse actions. Since the voice commands are consistent across applications, OfficeTALK maximises application independence, allowing the user to quickly become productive with many applications.

LASERFORM LAW

Head Office: 9-11 Princess Street, Knutsford, Cheshire WA16 6BY

Tel: 01565 755154
Fax: 01565 633807
E-Mail: admin@laserform.co.uk
Helpdesk available
Normal Office Hours (0171 333 0666)

Contact: Alison Bagnall, Kestrel Accounts Manager
Contact: Ian Perry, Sales Manager (Forms)
Contact: Barry Hawley-Green, Managing Director

Business established in 1989
No. of Directors 4
No. of Staff: 20
Target firm size: Any / All

PRODUCT DETAILS
Intelliforms

Environments Supported
Novell
Windows 3.x - Native
Windows 95 - 16 bit
Windows 95 - 32 bit
Windows NT

Application
Electronic Publishing - Legal Forms

Kestrel Solicitors Accounts

Environments Supported
DOS
Novell
Windows 3.x - Native
Windows 95 - 16 bit
Windows NT

Application
Accounting - Accounts & Time Recording

Know-How Case Management

Environments Supported
Windows 3.x - Native
Windows 95 - 16 bit
Windows 95 - 32 bit

Application
Case Management - Conveyancing
Case Management - Debt Collection
Case Management - General Purpose
Case Management - Probate

Most companies get letters through their doors...
We get trophies through our windows.

Society for Computers
and
Law Award

Electronic legal forms software

*Laserform M.D. Barry Hawley-Green
receives his award from Lord Woolf.*

*Announcing - Laserform Law win the prestigious award
from the Society for Computers & Law for
'Innovative software which has **most benefited** the legal profession"*

If you would like a FREE trial or more information please call Ian Perry
on 01565 755154 or return this form by fax on 01565 633807.

Name _____   Position _____

Address _____   Post Code _____

DX _____ Telephone _____   Fax _____

Most practices choose Laserform

Laserform Electronic Legal Forms

Environments Supported
Character-Based Terminal Emulation
DOS
Novell
UNIX
VAX/VMS
Windows 3.x - Native
Windows 95 - 16 bit
Windows 95 - 32 bit
Windows NT

Application
Electronic Publishing - Legal Forms

Company Profile
Laserform Law work very closely with the UK legal profession and specialise in quality legal software. Our range includes the electronic legal forms system, intelligent legal forms, Kestrel solicitors accounts and Case Management. All our products are written to Microsoft standards and are available under Windows, Windows 95 and Windows NT. As members of the Computer Software and Services Association all our employees abide by their code of conduct. We are also members of the Association of Legal Technology Suppliers. Laserform Law have over 1, 700 practices currently using our products and we pride ourselves on having a very large independent user group who give advice and guidance on many aspects of our business.

LAW COMPUTER SERVICES LTD

Head Office: 103 London Road, Mitcham, Surrey CR4 2JA

Tel: 0181 648 5641
Fax: 0181 646 0191
Helpdesk available
Normal office hours

Contact: Colin Kilbride
Contact: Lisa Preuveneers, Director

Business established in 1982
No. of Directors 3
No. of Staff: 6
Target firm size: Any / All

PRODUCT DETAILS
IntuITion - Speech Recognition Program
The Spoken Word - Word Processing by Voice

Environments Supported
DOS
Novell
Windows 3.x - CBT Emulation
Windows 3.x - Native
Windows 95 - 16 bit
Windows 95 - 32 bit
Windows NT

Application
Case Management - Conveyancing
Case Management - General Purpose
Miscellaneous - Other
Office Systems - Database - Clients and Contacts
Other

Company Profile
Originally a facility management company for a highly successful legal practice, Law Computer Services Ltd offer advice and assistance in applying the latest computer technology. Law Computer Services Ltd are at the very forefront of speech recognition and we specialise in the practical application of using computers by voice. Our unique product knowledge, unmatched experience, complete customer consideration and a first class level of training without equal in the UK today have given LCS a quite enviable market position and an extensive and high quality client base.

Law Systems Ltd

Head Office: 8-10 Berkeley Vale, Falmouth, Cornwall TR11 3PH

Tel: 01326 317529
Fax: 01326 313448
E-Mail: compuserve 100331, 3157
Helpdesk available
9.00am -5.15pm

Contact: David Stonehouse, Managing Director

Business established in 1992
No. of Directors 2
No. of Staff: 3
Target firm size: Any / All

Product Details
Probate Plus

Environments Supported
DOS

Application
Accounting - Estate Accounts

Company Profile
Law Systems Ltd supply a software system known as Probate Plus which is designed to produce Probate/ Administration Accounts. The system requires DOS version 3.3 or later as the operating system for an IBM PC compatible computer.

Lawbase Legal Systems

Head Office: Charlotte House, 87 Little Ealing Lane, London W5 4EH

Tel: 0181 840 9994
Fax: 0181 566 5523
Helpdesk available
9.00am - 5.30pm

Contact: Wyn Melville-Jones

Business established in 1984
No. of Directors 6
No. of Staff: 7
Target firm size: Medium, Large

Product Details
Lawbase Practice Database

Environments Supported
Character-Based Terminal Emulation
Novell
UNIX
VAX/VMS
Windows 3.x - Native
Windows 95 - 16 bit

Application
Accounting - Accounts & Time Recording
Calculators - Child Support Act
Calculators - Expense of Time
Case Management - Civil Litigation
Case Management - Conveyancing
Case Management - Criminal
Case Management - Debt Collection
Case Management - General Purpose
Case Management - Personal Injury
Case Management - Probate
Case Management - Road Traffic Act Claims
Case Management - Uninsured Loss Recovery
Document Assembly Systems - General Purpose
Document Assembly Systems - Letter Writing
Document Assembly Systems - Will Drafting
Electronic Publishing - Legal Forms
Legal Aid Franchising
Office Systems - Database - Clients and Contacts
Office Systems - Database - Marketing and Mailing
Office Systems - E-mail and shared Diary

Company Profile

Lawbase specialises in packaged and tailored software for: lawyers in private practice; legal departments of financial institutions; legal departments of other companies. Lawbase systems are ready-to-use: procedures, precedents, forms, correspondence and reports are all provided. This ensures rapid and cost-effective implementation. The software may be tailored by the user or by Lawbase before and after implementation. Case management systems for all types of legal work are integrated with a database, accounting and time-recording. Case management performs time-recording automatically as a by-product of producing work. Accounting software meets the needs of modern practice. All new Lawbase systems are available with a choice of Word and WordPerfect libraries. Lawbase software runs on stand-alone PCs, on Windows NT or Pathworks networks and on UNIX systems. (Not every package currently runs in every environment.) Complete "turn-key" solutions - cabling, hardware, software, installation, training and support - are provided. Any element of this service can be supplied independently. Lawbase software was first published in 1984 and has since been supplied to over 300 firms of solicitors and to the legal departments of banks, building societies and insurance companies amongst others.

LAWTEL CENTAUR COMMUNICATIONS

Head Office: St Giles House, 50 Poland Street, London WIV 4AX

Tel: 0171 287 9800
Fax: 1071 287 8483
Helpdesk available
9.00am - 6.00pm

Contact: Rachel Lesiter, Sales & Marketing Manager

Business established in 1980
No. of Directors 12
No. of Staff: 550
Target firm size: Any / All

PRODUCT DETAILS
Lawtel - Electronic Publishing

Environments Supported
Character-Based Terminal Emulation
DOS
Novell
Windows 3.x - Native
Windows 95 - 16 bit

Application
Electronic Publishing - Online Information Services

Company Profile

LAWTEL is the UK's leading on-line legal database with the fastest, easiest, most intuitive access to the law. Available via the Internet or direct dial, LAWTEL is updated every 24 hours to ensure lawyers are kept right up to date with the very latest developments. LAWTEL databases include: Case Law, Personal Injury, Practice Directions, Statutory Instruments, Statute Summaries, Statute Commencement Dates, Parliamentary Bills, Green & White Papers and Articles Index; plus: Daily Update, European Law, Research Bureau, Legal Directories (Havers & Waterlow's), LAWTEL Library Service and Company Searches (Infocheck). LAWTEL's price structure means that users only pay for the information retrieved.

LINK

Head Office: 28-33 Cato Street, London W1H 5HS

Tel: 0171 396 9292
Fax: 0171 396 9300
E-Mail: nigel_armitage@link.org
Helpdesk available
9.00am - 5.30pm

Contact: Nigel Armitage, Business Manager

No. of Staff: 12

Target firm size: Any / All

PRODUCT DETAILS
Legal Information Network - on-line system

Environments Supported
Macintosh System 7.x
Windows 3.x - CBT Emulation
Windows 3.x - Native
Windows 95 - 16 bit
Windows 95 - 32 bit
Windows NT

Application
Electronic Publishing - Online Information Services
Office Systems - E-mail and shared Diary

Company Profile
Link is part of Legalease Ltd and is the largest on-line system for the legal profession outside North America with in excess of 7, 500 users. The system is closed and secure. 80% of Link's services are free to use - there is no registration fee, no subscription and sending e-mail is free of charge. The system has a number of value added services, e.g. company search reports and electronic legal forms available by e-mail. Link also produces a high quality hard copy publication entitled "On-Line In Print" which is aimed at the legal profession and covers many IT/law-related issues. This publication has a monthly circulation of 30, 000 lawyers. Editor: Nigel Armitage.

LONDON BRIDGE SYSTEMS

Head Office: New London Bridge House, 7th Floor, 25 London Bridge Street, London SE1 9SG

Tel: 0171 403 1333
Fax: 0171 403 8981
Helpdesk available
Normal office hours

Contact: Declan Evans, Sales Executive
Contact: James Reid, Director

Business established in 1985
No. of Directors 4
No. of Staff: 60
Target firm size: Any / All

PRODUCT DETAILS
Lawfiler

Environments Supported
DOS
Novell
UNIX
Windows 3.x - Native
Windows 95 - 16 bit
Windows NT

Application
Case Management - Civil Litigation
Case Management - Conveyancing
Case Management - Criminal
Case Management - Debt Collection
Case Management - General Purpose
Case Management - Personal Injury
Case Management - Probate
Case Management - Road Traffic Act Claims
Case Management - Uninsured Loss Recovery
Document Assembly Systems - General Purpose
Document Assembly Systems - Letter Writing
Information Management - Document Management
Legal Aid Franchising
Miscellaneous - Other
Office Systems - Database - Clients and Contacts
Office Systems - Database - Marketing and Mailing
Office Systems - E-mail and shared Diary
Office Systems - Fee Earner Desktop

TRIAL/400

Environments Supported
Character-Based Terminal Emulation
Windows 3.x - CBT Emulation

Application
Accounting - Accounts & Time Recording
Office Systems - Database - Clients and Contacts
Office Systems - Database - Marketing and Mailing
Office Systems - Fee Earner Desktop

Company Profile
London Bridge Systems is a software house based in the centre of London, specialising in the provision of high quality software and associated services. Products include the Trial Family of Accounting Systems, which are available to suit all types and sizes of firms, from a sole practitioner on a stand alone PC through to international law firms operating in several offices across the world. London Bridge Group also provides a comprehensive range of Fee Earner Support systems. These are all based on the Lawfiler software, which is a modern Windows based product to improve both fee earner productivity and quality. The system includes a client database, matter database, simple time recording (with interface to update accounts systems), integration to word processing for automatic document production and a user defined case manager that can support all work types from criminal to conveyancing. Additional modules are available for litigation support and document image processing and management.

MANAGEMENT INTERFACE LIMITED (MIL)

Head Office: Warlies Park House, Horseshoe Hill, Upshire, Waltham Abbey, Essex EN9 3SL

Tel: 01992 788288
Fax: 01992 788488

Contact: Roger George
Contact: Chris Relph

PRODUCT DETAILS
Incontrol

Environments Supported
DOS
Novell
UNIX
Windows 95 - 16 bit
Windows 95 - 32 bit

Application
Accounting - Accounts & Time Recording
Case Management - Debt Collection
Case Management - General Purpose
Case Management - Mortgage Repossessions
Case Management - Probate
Case Management - Uninsured Loss Recovery
Office Systems - Time Recording
Office Systems - Word Processing

"Information Technology is now recognised as a fundamental business tool. It can help reduce costs, improve productivity and encourage a greater sharing of knowledge and information."

Company Profile

Established in 1981, Management Interface Ltd (MIL) is one of the premier legal system companies in the UK. We provide an integrated range of both stand-alone and multi-user systems, and our policy of development and expansion ensures we remain in the forefront of system applications for the legal profession. In keeping with the need to maintain the very highest standards MIL has obtained the ISO 9002 Quality Registration (formerly BS5750). There are now some 1300 Solicitor firms using our systems (PC, network and multi-user based) for Accounts, Debt Recovery, Litigation Support, WordPerfect etc. We are a "listed" Law Society Supplier and our clients benefit from our on-line system support throughout every working day. All MIL systems offer great flexibility and have been specifically designed to expand as the requirements of each firm dictates; our objective is to match the latest technology with high quality software, allowing us to provide comprehensive tailor-made solutions to suit client requirements. MIL's success has been built on our integrated systems approach for the professional legal office; this provides a central database of client and accounting information irrespective of the support systems implementation, and eliminates duplication of information across systems. It also ensures an easy means of installation and operation, whatever the size and volume of work. However, our systems are designed to allow firms to implement the applications in a phased manner in line with priorities and resources. Hardware, Software, Maintenance, Training and Project Management are all provided from a single source. This ensures a speedy response to queries and obviates the need to establish who is responsible.

MERIDIAN LEGAL SYSTEMS LIMITED

Head Office: 5-6 Maiden Lane, Stamford, Lincolnshire PE9 2AZ

Tel: 01780 482795
Fax: 01780 65322

Contact: Graham Currie, Director

Business established in 1978
No. of Directors 4
No. of Staff: 10

PRODUCT DETAILS
Solpak For Windows

Environments Supported
Novell
Windows 3.x - CBT Emulation
Windows 3.x - Native
Windows 95 - 16 bit
Windows 95 - 32 bit
Windows NT

Application
Accounting - Accounts & Time Recording
Calculators - Child Support Act
Calculators - Employment Loss
Calculators - Expense of Time
Calculators - Social Security Benefits
Case Management - Civil Litigation
Case Management - Conveyancing
Case Management - Criminal
Case Management - Debt Collection
Case Management - General Purpose
Case Management - Personal Injury
Case Management - Probate
Case Management - Road Traffic Act Claims
Case Management - Uninsured Loss Recovery
Information Management - Document Management
Information Management - Know-How
Information Management - Library Systems
Information Management - Text Retrieval Software
Legal Aid Franchising
Office Systems - Database - Clients and Contacts
Office Systems - Database - Marketing and Mailing
Office Systems - Desk-top Faxing
Office Systems - E-mail and shared Diary
Office Systems - Fee Earner Desktop

Company Profile

The first of a new generation of computer products for the legal profession, which are entirely Windows based (Windows 3.1 and Windows 95). The system provides a totally integrated business solution incorporating Windows functionality for ease of use by partners, fee-earners, support staff and accounts staff alike. Designed by financial, legal and computer professionals with years of experience, to meet practice management standards, BS5750, and the demands of LAB franchising specification. The central base of client matter related information permeates through to the accounts, time costing, word processing spread sheet and the entire range of legal support modules. As you would expect, the system is multi-user, multi-branch and multi-company. Being Windows based, you will be provided with the added benefits of a genuine multi-tasking operating system. The products are offered either as a software only solution or, a complete package if you prefer a single source of supply. The user base, is both widespread and wide-ranging in size and style. As such our products will meet the requirements of the majority of firms in England and Wales regardless of size. New standards are now in place, with the introduction of high powered PCs and PC networks able to operate in a Windows environment. Solpak for Windows provides exciting new standards in legal application software, to complement this new generation of office automation.

MicroTRIAL Ltd

Head Office: The Old Station, Main Street, Aslockton, Nottingham, Nottinghamshire NG13 9AB

Tel: 01949 851109
Fax: 01949 851235
Helpdesk available
Normal office hours

Contact: Julie Ellis, Senior Systems Consultant

Business established in 1987
No. of Directors 2
No. of Staff: 3
Target firm size: Any / All

PRODUCT DETAILS
MicroTRIAL

Environments Supported
DOS
Windows 3.x - CBT Emulation
Windows 3.x - Native
Windows 95 - 16 bit
Windows NT

Application
Accounting - Accounts & Time Recording
Accounting - Accounts (no Time Recording)
Accounting - Trust Accounts
Case Management - Civil Litigation
Case Management - Conveyancing
Case Management - Criminal
Case Management - Debt Collection
Case Management - Personal Injury
Case Management - Probate
Case Management - Road Traffic Act Claims
Case Management - Uninsured Loss Recovery

Company Profile

MicroTRIAL Ltd is a specialist computer software company formed in 1987, dedicated to providing computerised solutions for the legal profession. MicroTRIAL's fully integrated accounting and time recording system is continuously revised and updated in response to user feedback and fully conforms to Law Society and Legal Aid Franchise requirements. The system offers extensive reporting capabilities with full management information tools to monitor areas of profitability and productivity. A credit control facility is part of the suite of programs and offers comprehensive reporting and chasing of aged-debts with personalised statement production. Time can be recorded either manually or by use of a palm-top computer and caters for both fee-earner and legal aid rates with full reporting and billing guides. MicroTRIAL software is available as either a single-user or multi-user system and will run on any PC compatible machine under all levels of DOS, Novell and Windows. MicroTRIAL will also link to DPS front office systems for the purpose of displaying ledger details for the associated case. MicroTRIAL is a proven system which has been successfully installed into legal firms varying in size from the sole practitioner to the multi-fee-earner practices, spread both nationally and internationally.

MOUNTAIN SOFTWARE

Head Office: Withambrook Park, Grantham, Lincolnshire NG31 9ST

Tel: 01476 73718
Fax: 01476 590563
Helpdesk available
Normal office hours

Contact: Steve Kendrick, Sales Director

Business established in 1976
No. of Directors 3
No. of Staff: 17
Target firm size: Small, Medium

PRODUCT DETAILS
Conveyancing Support Software

Environments Supported
DOS
Novell
Windows 3.x - Native
Windows 95 - 16 bit

Application
Case Management - Conveyancing

Debt Recovery

Environments Supported
DOS
Novell
Windows 3.x - CBT Emulation
Windows 95 - 16 bit

Application
Case Management - Debt Collection

Deeds Storage

Environments Supported
DOS
Windows 3.x - Native
Windows 95 - 16 bit

Application
Miscellaneous - Other

Extended Client/Matter Database

Environments Supported
DOS
Novell
Windows 3.x - Native
Windows 95 - 16 bit

Application
Case Management - General Purpose
Office Systems - Database - Clients and Contacts

Fee Recovery

Environments Supported
DOS
Novell
Windows 3.x - Native
Windows 95 - 16 bit

Application
Case Management - Debt Collection

Investment Storage

Environments Supported
DOS
Novell
Windows 3.x - Native
Windows 95 - 16 bit

Application
Financial Services - General
Office Systems - E-mail and shared Diary

Legal Accounts & Time Keeping

Environments Supported
DOS
Novell
Windows 3.x - CBT Emulation
Windows 95 - 16 bit

Application
Accounting - Accounts & Time Recording
Accounting - Accounts (no Time Recording)

Matrimonial Support System

Environments Supported
Novell
Windows 3.x - Native
Windows 95 - 16 bit

Application
Case Management - Matrimonial

Payroll

Environments Supported
DOS
Windows 3.x - CBT Emulation
Windows 95 - 16 bit

Application
Miscellaneous - Other

Personnel Records

Environments Supported
DOS
Novell
Windows 3.x - Native
Windows 95 - 16 bit

Application
Miscellaneous - Other

Probate Support System

Environments Supported
Novell
Windows 3.x - Native
Windows 95 - 16 bit

Application
Case Management - Probate

Wills Storage

Environments Supported
DOS
Novell
Windows 3.x - Native
Windows 95 - 16 bit

Application
Miscellaneous - Other

Company Profile

At Mountain Software, we are well into our second decade of providing computerised solutions to the legal profession. Our systems operate in hundreds of legal practices throughout England & Wales, the Channel Islands and the Isle of Man. These organisations range in size from sole practitioners up to companies with over 100 fee-earners. The introduction of Mountain Software's Extended Client/Matter Database heralds a breakthrough for the company into 4GL software. Initially developed to meet the requirements of the Legal Aid Board for Franchising, the database has been further extended to form the fulcrum of our software packages. It provides a seamless link between accounts, word processing, conveyancing and any other software packages. We believe that our commitment to excellence and our dedication to developing the best solutions for our customers, at realistic prices, make our products the most cost effective on the market, not only today but towards the 21st century. Mountain Software are a major supplier to solicitors firms that have achieved BS5750 accreditation.

MSG Computers

Head Office: The Summit, Castle Hill Terrace, Maidenhead, Berkshire SL6 4JP

Tel: 01628 71621
Fax: 01628 23953
E-Mail: compuserve:100552, 1355
Helpdesk available
Normal office hours

Contact: Nigel Lancaster, Director

Business established in 1982
No. of Directors 5
No. of Staff: 10
Target firm size: Any / All

Product Details
Solidus

Environments Supported
Character-Based Terminal Emulation
DOS
Novell
Windows 3.x - CBT Emulation
Windows 3.x - Native
Windows 95 - 16 bit
Windows 95 - 32 bit

Application
Accounting - Accounts & Time Recording
Case Management - Conveyancing
Case Management - Debt Collection
Case Management - Matrimonial
Case Management - Personal Injury
Document Assembly Systems - General Purpose
Document Assembly Systems - Letter Writing
Electronic Publishing - Legal Forms
Legal Aid Franchising
Office Systems - Database - Clients and Contacts
Office Systems - Database - Marketing and Mailing
Office Systems - Desk-top Faxing
Office Systems - E-mail and shared Diary

Company Profile

MSG Computers is a software and systems house specialising in the design and development of computer systems for the legal and allied professions. Their systems include straightforward client accounting and time recording, time-recording via fee-earner and hand-held/ portable computers, fully automated debt collection, fully automated conveyancing, litigation support, word processing, electronic forms origination. MSG is licensed by HM Land Registry and HMSO for the production of selected HMLR and Inland Revenue documents. MSG operates a comprehensive after-sales service and has a policy of continual development and enhancement.

Nexus Technology Limited

Head Office: Marlborough House, 82 Park Street, Camberley, Surrey GU15 3NY

Tel: 01276 686 900
Fax: 01276 686 901
E-Mail: 100726.2230@compuserve.com
Helpdesk available
9.00am - 5.00pm

Contact: Ian Brown, Sales Director

Business established in 1991
No. of Directors 2
No. of Staff: 20
Target firm size: Small, Medium, Large

Product Details
CASEnotes

Environments Supported
Macintosh System 7.x
UNIX
Windows 3.x - Native
Windows 95 - 32 bit
Windows NT

Application
Case Management - Civil Litigation
Case Management - Conveyancing
Case Management - Criminal
Case Management - Debt Collection
Case Management - General Purpose
Case Management - Personal Injury
Case Management - Probate
Case Management - Road Traffic Act Claims
Case Management - Uninsured Loss Recovery
Information Management - Document Management
Office Systems - Database - Clients and Contacts
Office Systems - Database - Marketing and Mailing
Office Systems - Desk-top Faxing
Office Systems - E-mail and shared Diary
Office Systems - Fee Earner Desktop

Norwel Computer Services Ltd

Head Office: Parkway House, Palatine Road, Manchester M22 4DB

Tel: 0161 945 3511
Fax: 0161 946 0231
E-Mail: ds@norwel.demon.co.uk
Helpdesk available
Normal office hours

Contact: Deborah Stevenson, Marketing Manager
Contact: Marcus Macleod, Businesss Manager (London)

Business established in 1972
No. of Directors 4
No. of Staff: 30
Target firm size: Any / All

Product Details
Norwel Case Management

Environments Supported
UNIX
Windows 3.x - Native

Application
Case Management - Conveyancing
Case Management - Debt Collection
Case Management - General Purpose
Office Systems - Database - Clients and Contacts
Office Systems - Database - Marketing and Mailing
Office Systems - Desk-top Faxing
Office Systems - E-mail and shared Diary
Office Systems - Fee Earner Desktop

Norwel Conveyancing

Environments Supported
Character-Based Terminal Emulation
Novell
Windows 3.x - Native

Application
Case Management - Conveyancing

Norwel Debt Collection

Environments Supported
Character-Based Terminal Emulation
Novell
Windows 3.x - Native

Application
Case Management - Debt Collection

Norwel Practice Management

Environments Supported
Character-Based Terminal Emulation
UNIX
Windows 3.x - Native
Windows NT

Application
Accounting - Accounts & Time Recording
Accounting - Estate Accounts
Accounting - Trust Accounts
Case Management - Conveyancing
Case Management - Debt Collection
Case Management - General Purpose
Electronic Publishing - Legal Forms
Financial Services - Portfolio Management
Information Management - Document Management
Office Systems - Database - Clients and Contacts
Office Systems - Database - Marketing and Mailing
Office Systems - E-mail and shared Diary
Office Systems - Fee Earner Desktop

Norwel Trust Accounting & Portfolio Management

Environments Supported
Character-Based Terminal Emulation
Novell
Windows 3.x - Native

Application
Financial Services - Portfolio Management

Company Profile

Norwel is one of the leading IT suppliers to the legal
profession and has a substantial user base amongst both
City and regional firms. Norwel has developed a range of
software products designed to support almost every aspect
of work in a solicitor's practice. Solely dedicated to the
legal market, the Norwel team has expertise in networking,
systems integration, training and consultancy which ensures
successful implementations.

OXFORD LAW AND COMPUTING LTD

Head Office: The Old Vicarage, East Hagbourne, Didcot, Oxon OX11 9LP

Tel: 01235 510396
Fax: 01235 510273
E-Mail: 100016.3551@compuserve.com
or RJBOxLaw@msn.com
Helpdesk available
Normal office hours

Contact: Richard Brockbank, Managing Director

Business established in 1988
No. of Directors 4
No. of Staff: 4
Target firm size: Small, Medium, Large, Local
Government, Other, Any / All

PRODUCT DETAILS
Openlaw Document Listing Software - Image version

Environments Supported
Novell
Windows 3.x - Native
Windows 95 - 16 bit
Windows NT

Application
Litigation Support - Document Listing Software
Litigation Support - Image-based Discovery Systems
Office Systems - Scanning Imaging and OCR

Openlaw Document Listing Software (for the smaller firm)

Environments Supported
DOS
Novell
Windows 3.x - Native
Windows 95 - 16 bit
Windows NT

Application
Litigation Support - Document Listing Software

Openlaw Know-how System

Environments Supported
Novell
Windows 3.x - Native
Windows 95 - 16 bit
Windows 95 - 32 bit
Windows NT

Application
Information Management - Know-How
Office Systems - Scanning Imaging and OCR

Openlaw Office Partner

Environments Supported
Novell
Windows 3.x - Native
Windows 95 - 16 bit
Windows 95 - 32 bit
Windows NT

Application
Case Management - Civil Litigation
Case Management - General Purpose
Document Assembly Systems - General Purpose
Document Assembly Systems - Letter Writing
Information Management - Document Management
Office Systems - Database - Clients and Contacts
Office Systems - Database - Marketing and Mailing
Office Systems - E-mail and shared Diary
Office Systems - Quality Management/Client Care Steps
Office Systems - Scanning Imaging and OCR
Office Systems - Word Processing

Openlaw Perfect Office Partner

Environments Supported
Novell
Windows 3.x - Native
Windows 95 - 16 bit
Windows 95 - 32 bit
Windows NT

Application
Case Management - Civil Litigation
Case Management - General Purpose
Document Assembly Systems - General Purpose
Document Assembly Systems - Letter Writing
Information Management - Document Management
Information Management - Know-How
Office Systems - Database - Clients and Contacts
Office Systems - Database - Marketing and Mailing
Office Systems - Desk-top Faxing
Office Systems - E-mail and shared Diary
Office Systems - Quality Management/Client Care Steps
Office Systems - Scanning Imaging and OCR

Company Profile

We specialise in all aspects of the review, strategy, planning, development, implementation, training, use and management of IT in law firms. We offer consultancy and/ or solutions. Where appropriate we will work in conjunction with your existing advisers (e.g. on marketing). We have worked for the Law Society and firms ranging from very large City and Scottish to small provincial firms. Because of our professional backgrounds (in law and accountancy) we can understand and appreciate the working needs of staff in all areas and at all levels, and can then apply, recommend or supply the appropriate IT solutions. Because we have day-to-day experience of the latest tools and technology we can usually link new systems in to existing proprietary systems and combine and customise standard tools to assist with most legal office tasks. Our philosophy is to encourage the development of applications using best of breed components from the industry majors (Microsoft, Novell, IBM/Lotus, Oracle, Systems Union etc). Areas of special expertise include letter-writing systems built around a contacts database, bespoke case management systems, marketing and conflict databases, litigation support systems (with or without images), electronic transfer of data from existing systems (financial and other) and sophisticated financial analysis and reporting, with appropriate presentation formats for financial managers and partners. We have many accreditations including Lotus Business Partners, Microsoft Solutions Providers, Oracle Business Partners and Watermark Imaging Businessware Partners.

OYEZ LEGAL SOFTWARE

Head Office: Oyez House, 7 Spa Road, London SE16 3QQ

Tel: 0171 232 1000
Fax: 0171 231 7393
Normal office hours

Contact: Paul Cossey, Director of Legal Software

Business established in 1888
No. of Directors 8
No. of Staff: 550
Target firm size: Any / All

PRODUCT DETAILS
Forms Software

Environments Supported
Windows 3.x - Native

Application
Electronic Publishing - Legal Forms

Wills Software

Environments Supported
DOS

Application
Document Assembly Systems - Will Drafting

Company Profile
Oyez Forms produces a broad range of Oyez's market-leading forms quickly and easily direct from your own PC with this simple to use Windows based software. Oyez Forms on disk have been created in conjunction with our team of legal experts to ensure that forms comply with all current legislation. Oyez Wills is an easy to use software package that saves as much as 50% of will-making time, simplifies and reduces record keeping, produces invoices and is fully intelligent with no "cut and paste" paragraphs.

PC DOCS (UK) LIMITED

Head Office: 11-13 Capricorn Centre, Cranes Farm Road, Basildon, Essex SS14 3JJ

Tel: 01268 270601
Fax: 01268 270602
E-Mail: pcdocs@quintec.co.uk
Helpdesk available
Normal office hours

Contact: Tom Lee, Business Manager

Business established in 1992
No. of Directors 4
No. of Staff: 40
Target firm size: Any / All

PRODUCT DETAILS
DOCS Open Document Management System

Environments Supported
Windows 3.x - Native
Windows 95 - 16 bit

Application
Document Assembly Systems - General Purpose
Document Assembly Systems - Letter Writing
Document Assembly Systems - Will Drafting
Information Management - Document Management
Information Management - Know-How
Information Management - Library Systems
Information Management - Text Retrieval Software

Company Profile
PC DOCS OPEN is a Windows and SQL based document management system which utilises an open architecture and allows for increased integration of front and back office systems. PC DOCS OPEN supports SQL databases such as Microsoft SQL Server, Oracle and Sybase and runs on Novell, Lan Manger, and Banyan operating systems. PC DOCS OPEN is integrated with word processing applications, spreadsheets, E-mail packages, and Imaging Packages. PC DOCS OPEN brings increased efficiency to individuals and workgroups by organising and controlling the documents and files on your local and wide area networks. With PC DOCS OPEN, documents can be stored, tracked, retrieved, archived or deleted using a variety of criteria including: Author, Document type, Client, Matter, Keywords or Full Text. Other features include: Audit trails, Time Tracking and PC DOCS Mobile, which provides notebook users with a fully functional document management solution while they are away from the office. PC DOCS (UK) is part of QUINTEC INTERNATIONAL. See also associated company, CMS OPEN.

PEAPOD SOLUTIONS LIMITED

Head Office: Shirley Lodge, 470 London Road, Slough, Berks SL3 8QY

Tel: 01753 581600
Fax: 01753 581501
E-Mail: sales@peapod.co.uk
Helpdesk available
Normal office hours

Contact: Ian Wimbush, Managing Director

Business established in 1994
No. of Directors 3
No. of Staff: 14
Target firm size: Small, Medium

PRODUCT DETAILS
Accounts & Time Recording Packages

DPS - Document Processing System

Environments Supported
Novell
Windows NT

Application
Case Management - General Purpose

Network Management Products

PrintaForm

Environments Supported
Novell
Windows NT

Application
Electronic Publishing - Legal Forms

Company Profile

We are specialists in the legal office providing networked solutions for fee-earners and secretarial/support staff. Running under Novell's Netware, MS Windows NT, client/server and/or Microsoft's peer-to-peer operating enviromments. Our solutions include DPS, the leading Case Management software, PrintaForm, our own legal forms software, as well as a choice of two Accounts and Time Recording packages. These are complemented by a range of office applications software including Word for Windows, WordPerfect for Windows and Office 95. We provide complete networked or software only solutions incorporating proven software products, working with you to design a solution that fits your business today and will provide a long term strategy. We provide all the services using our own trained staff from cabling and installation to training and ongoing support. As a Microsoft Solutions provider we are required to keep our staff trained and certified. Our aim is to make your IT investment assist you in your business success. Our one stop support agreement covers all aspects of after sales service giving our customers peace of mind.

PERFECT SOFTWARE LTD

Head Office: Tondu Enterprise Centre, Bridgend, Mid Glamorgan CF32 9BS

Tel: 01656 720071
Helpdesk available
0374 806204 (8.00am - 8.00pm)

Contact: Patrick Carmody, Director

Business established in 1992
No. of Directors 2
No. of Staff: 5

PRODUCT DETAILS
Perfect Books - Accounts

Environments Supported
DOS
Windows 3.x - Native

Application
Accounting - Accounts (no Time Recording)

Perfect Books - Database

Environments Supported
DOS
Windows 3.x - Native

Application
Office Systems - Database - Clients and Contacts

Perfect Books - Time Recording

Environments Supported
DOS
Windows 3.x - Native

Application
Office Systems - Time Recording

Company Profile

Perfect Software specialises in providing accounts and practice management software for smaller firms and for sole practitioners. The Perfect Software team have a combined total of over 30 years experience in developing and using quality legal software. The latest product, Perfect Books Two, is designed to provide a reliable and comprehensive system which is really easy to use and therefore suitable for smaller firms. All the standard functions (interest calculation, bank reconciliation and VAT variations) are included. We live up to our name by supporting our rapidly expanding user base on all aspects of accounting and practice management software. For example, we operate an 8.00 am to 8.00 pm six-day helpline, always available to answer clients' book-keeping and computer queries. And we are committed to support any changes in requirements for accounts rules compliance, legal aid franchising and practice management standards. With networking and database, multi-user and multi-platform, this provides a perfect solution for accounting and practice management in small and medium sized firms.

Perfect makes Practice

Accounting to Law Society rules for the smaller practice and sole practitioner

Perfect Books has improved the accounting and practice management of over two hundred firms countrywide and could do the same for you.

The software is designed specifically for smaller practices and sole practitioners by Perfect Software Ltd who specialise only in legal software. The system meets present Law Society rules and our policy of continuing development will ensure that the software continues to meet the needs of the profession.

Perfect Books is:-

- ✔ easy for you to install and set up
- ✔ easy for you to use
- ✔ easy for you to understand

Perfect Books support is as close as your telephone from 9.0 am to 6.0 pm, Monday to Saturday.

Perfect Books is outstanding value for money - **full legal accounting for a single fee earner practice at just £575, including first year support and £100 for each additional fee earner** (plus VAT).

Some of our users comment on Perfect Books

"...It's marvellous - I was up and running in no time at all and now it's saving me time, all the time."
K. B. Thompson, Telford.

"Perfect Books brought my records under control much quicker than I expected .... it is so easy for me to use .... I could not do without it."
Ian Nelson, Portsmouth.

"I cannot fault the after sales service of Perfect Books. The support group are always good natured and patient with all my problems."
Arnold Rosen, London W1.

For further information and a free Perfect Books demonstration pack
Telephone 0181-546 7656 now !

Perfect Software ✔

Perfect Software Ltd.,
9 River Court,
Portsmouth Road,
Surbiton, Surrey KT6 4EY.
Telephone: 0181-546 7656

PILGRIM SYSTEMS PLC

Head Office: The City Business Centre, No. 2 London Wall Buildings, London Wall, London EC2M 5PP

Tel: 0171 382 9382
Fax: 0171 382 9728
E-Mail: 100272, 1322@compuserve.com
Helpdesk available
Normal office hours

Contact: Mike Smith, Sales Manager
Contact: Ron Goodman, Sales Manager
Contact: Ronnie Paton, Managing Director

Business established in 1978
No. of Directors 3
No. of Staff: 35
Target firm size: Any / All

PRODUCT DETAILS
Advocate (Accounts & Time Recording)

Environments Supported
Character-Based Terminal Emulation
DOS
Novell
UNIX
VAX/VMS
Windows 3.x - CBT Emulation

Application
Accounting - Accounts & Time Recording
Accounting - Estate Accounts
Office Systems - Fee Earner Desktop

Lawsoft Case Manager

Environments Supported
Windows 3.x - Native
Windows 95 - 32 bit
Windows NT

Application
Case Management - Civil Litigation
Case Management - Conveyancing
Case Management - Criminal
Case Management - Debt Collection
Case Management - General Purpose
Case Management - Matrimonial
Case Management - Mortgage Repossessions
Case Management - Personal Injury
Case Management - Probate
Case Management - Road Traffic Act Claims
Case Management - Uninsured Loss Recovery
Office Systems - Fee Earner Desktop

Lawsoft Contract & Marketing Manager

Environments Supported
Windows 3.x - Native
Windows 95 - 32 bit
Windows NT

Application
Office Systems - Database - Clients and Contacts
Office Systems - Database - Marketing and Mailing

Lawsoft Document Manager

Environments Supported
Windows 3.x - Native
Windows 95 - 32 bit
Windows NT

Application
Information Management - Document Management
Other

Lawsoft Practice Manager

Environments Supported
Windows 3.x - Native
Windows 95 - 32 bit
Windows NT

Application
Office Systems - Fee Earner Desktop

Company Profile

Since its formation in 1977 Pilgrim Systems has been a supplier of software to the legal profession. We have products designed to run on PC networks and multi-user systems under Unix. Pilgrim is an authorised Novell Network reseller and Microsoft Solutions Provider (Development Centre). We have produced the Lawsoft range of Windows products for PC networks which integrate with the Microsoft core applications (diary, E-Mail, WP, etc) to provide a seamless Windows operating environment. The Lawsoft modules include Practice Management (Accounts, Time Recording, Billing), Contact and Marketing Database, Document Management and Case Management. To support these products there is a global Report Generator, a Database and Screen Designer and Decision Maker to enable users to create their own workflow chains in Case Manager. Litigation Support allows images to be linked to a free text database. This enable lawyers to search voluminous documentation using given statements and immediately view the document images that meet the given criteria. We have recently supplied one of the largest systems of its kind, outside the US, to a law firm in London. Using the reporting routines the system can produce sorted lists of documents. Pilgrim provides a full range of technical services to support its product:

PRACCTICE

Head Office: Pracctice House, Twyford Road, Rotherwas, Hertfordshire HR2 6JR

Tel: 01432 351041
Fax: 01432 351042
E-Mail: sales@softleg.demon.co.uk

Contact: John Taylor, Managing Director

Business established in 1987
No. of Directors 2
No. of Staff: 15
Target firm size: Any / All

PRODUCT DETAILS
Pracctice Integrated

Environments Supported
DOS
Novell
Windows 3.x - Native
Windows 95 - 16 bit
Windows 95 - 32 bit
Windows NT

Application
Accounting - Accounts & Time Recording
Accounting - Accounts (no Time Recording)
Case Management - Civil Litigation
Case Management - Conveyancing
Case Management - Criminal
Case Management - Debt Collection
Case Management - General Purpose
Case Management - Personal Injury
Case Management - Probate
Electronic Publishing - Legal Forms
Electronic Publishing - Online Information Services
Legal Aid Franchising
Office Systems - Database - Clients and Contacts
Office Systems - Database - Marketing and Mailing
Office Systems - Desk-top Faxing
Office Systems - E-mail and shared Diary
Office Systems - Fee Earner Desktop

Company Profile

Pracctice is Law Society recognised and has a user base of more than 250 firms covering all areas of the UK. Powerful reporting facilities combine with practical, effective software design and expert implementation to provide comprehensive and effective systems. Our commitment to Windows NT and Windows 95 development in a fully integrated computing environment guarantees that your IT spend is an investment for the future. Our systems provide seamless integration of database, accounting and time recording information, whilst our report generator allows the user to control all aspects of reporting, extracting any type of information, deciding selection criteria and designing formats. We are a committed open systems supplier.

PROFESSIONAL PRODUCTIVITY SOLUTIONS

Head Office: The Old Bishops House, 44 Brook Street, Watlington, Oxford OX9 5JH

Tel: 01865 201801
Fax: 01685 201901
E-Mail: sales@ppslaw.co.uk
Helpdesk available
9.00am - 1.00pm & 2.00pm - 5.00pm

Contact: Nicholas Mcfarlane-Watts, Director Solicitor

Business established in 1987
No. of Directors 2
No. of Staff: 20
Target firm size: Small, Medium

PRODUCT DETAILS

Environments Supported
Macintosh System 7.x
Windows 3.x - Native
Windows 95 - 16 bit

Application
Accounting - Accounts & Time Recording
Accounting - Estate Accounts
Calculators - Expense of Time
Case Management - Conveyancing
Case Management - Debt Collection
Case Management - General Purpose
Case Management - Probate
Document Assembly Systems - General Purpose
Document Assembly Systems - Letter Writing
Document Assembly Systems - Will Drafting
Financial Services - General
Financial Services - Portfolio Management
Information Management - Document Management
Information Management - Know-How
Information Management - Library Systems
Information Management - Text Retrieval Software
Legal Aid Franchising
Litigation Support - Document Listing Software
Litigation Support - Image-based Discovery Systems
Miscellaneous - Other
Office Systems - Database - Clients and Contacts
Office Systems - Database - Marketing and Mailing
Office Systems - Desk-top Faxing
Office Systems - E-mail and shared Diary
Office Systems - Fee Earner Desktop
Other

Company Profile

Professional Productivity Solutions (PPS) was incorporated in 1987 to develop a new range of software for lawyers, taking advantage of the ease of use of the Apple Macintosh and later of Windows. At its first Barbican exhibition in 1988, PPS legal software was acclaimed as a major development "... technically sophisticated and very easy to operate ... years ahead of anything commercially available in this country" ("Solicitors Journal"). PPS attained PLC status in 1991 and went on to develop one of the widest ranges of legal software products in the UK. The company's products are developed to be modular, allowing a practice to start with a core system at a lower investment cost, and expandable, adding further modular products as demands require and budget permits, and building up into a complete integrated practice-wide system. Described in the "Journal of the Society for Computers and Law" as "the UK's leading Macintosh legal systems specialist", PPS now offers its products for both Apple Macintosh and Windows, including mixed networks of the two platforms. PPS has provided systems to practices nationwide, from Sussex to Tyne & Wear, and from Cornwall to Lincolnshire, with on-going support. The company is run by solicitors, and support personnel have legal qualifications or experience.

PROFESSIONAL TECHNOLOGY (UK) LTD

Head Office: 375 High Street, Rochester, Kent ME1 1EA

Tel: 01634 815517
Fax: 01634 829032
E-Mail: compuserve100020, 1371
Helpdesk available
9.30am - 5.30pm

Contact: Bob Chapman, Sales Director
Contact: James Dirks, Consultant

Business established in 1986
No. of Directors 2
No. of Staff: 6
Target firm size: Any / All

PRODUCT DETAILS
Quaestor

Environments Supported
Novell
Windows 3.x - Native
Windows 95 - 16 bit
Windows 95 - 32 bit
Windows NT

Application
Accounting - Accounts & Time Recording
Accounting - Accounts (no Time Recording)
Case Management - Debt Collection
Case Management - Road Traffic Act Claims
Case Management - Uninsured Loss Recovery
Document Assembly Systems - General Purpose
Document Assembly Systems - Letter Writing
Document Assembly Systems - Will Drafting
Electronic Publishing - Legal Forms
Information Management - Document Management
Information Management - Know-How
Information Management - Library Systems
Information Management - Text Retrieval Software
Legal Aid Franchising
Miscellaneous - Other
Office Systems - Desk-top Faxing
Office Systems - E-mail and shared Diary
Office Systems - Fee Earner Desktop

Seriatim

Environments Supported
DOS
Novell
Windows 3.x - Native
Windows 95 - 16 bit
Windows 95 - 32 bit
Windows NT

Application
Accounting - Accounts & Time Recording
Accounting - Accounts (no Time Recording)
Case Management - Debt Collection
Case Management - Road Traffic Act Claims
Case Management - Uninsured Loss Recovery
Document Assembly Systems - General Purpose
Document Assembly Systems - Letter Writing
Document Assembly Systems - Will Drafting
Electronic Publishing - Legal Forms
Information Management - Document Management
Information Management - Know-How
Information Management - Library Systems
Information Management - Text Retrieval Software
Legal Aid Franchising
Miscellaneous - Other
Office Systems - Desk-top Faxing
Office Systems - E-mail and shared Diary
Office Systems - Fee Earner Desktop

Company Profile
Professional Technology has, as its primary objective, the provision of computer solutions of the highest quality to the legal profession. The software is capable of running across a wide spectrum. The QUAESTOR/SERIATIM System is modular in design and includes client and matter database, accounting, time recording, calculation of interest, cheque writing, nominal export (can export information to spreadsheets), legal aid budgeting-workflow management and litigation case management. The system is designed around a unique multi-function posting routine which allows entries like bills, transfer, petty cash and client/office banking to be handled without the need to change screens or functions. It also makes use of drop-down menus and pop-up windows to assist the user in switching from one task to another and is capable of linking to other leading software for conveyancing, criminal litigation, wills register, personal injury, matrimonial and cost drafting. The system has the ability to export data to most other systems. All information is password protected, both recognising and integrating the Law Society's accounting rules for client related entries and supporting privacy and protection for sensitive information within the nominal ledgers and fee earners' details of the practice. The staff have all dealt with lawyers for many years and are trained to act as advisors to their clients. They try to make them understand and appreciate the benefits of modern technology, particularly with regard to the management information that computers can so easily provide.

Quill Computer Systems Ltd

Head Office: Barclay House, 35 Whitworth Street West, Manchester M1 5NG

Tel: 0161 236 2910
Fax: 0161 237 1131
Helpdesk available
9.00am - 5.30pm

Contact: David Phillips, Northern Sales Manager
Contact: Peter Dye, Southern Sales Manager

Business established in 1978
No. of Directors 3
No. of Staff: 24
Target firm size: Any/All

Product Details

Environments Supported
Character-Based Terminal Emulation
DOS
Novell
UNIX
Windows 3.x - CBT Emulation
Windows 3.x - Native
Windows 95 - 16 bit
Windows 95 - 32 bit
Windows NT

Application
Accounting - Accounts & Time Recording
Accounting - Accounts (no Time Recording)
Case Management - Conveyancing
Case Management - Criminal
Case Management - Debt Collection
Case Management - General Purpose
Case Management - Landlord & Tenant
Case Management - Matrimonial
Case Management - Personal Injury
Case Management - Road Traffic Act Claims
Case Management - Uninsured Loss Recovery
Document Assembly Systems - General Purpose
Document Assembly Systems - Letter Writing
Legal Aid Franchising
Office Systems - Database - Clients and Contacts
Office Systems - Database - Marketing and Mailing
Office Systems - Desk-top Faxing
Office Systems - E-mail and shared Diary
Office Systems - Fee Earner Desktop

Company Profile

Quill Computer Systems was one of the pioneers of specialist software for solicitors and the company's steady growth and continued success is owed to its on-going development of relevant, easy-to-use systems to meet the evolving needs of the profession. As well as keeping pace with the latest technology, Quill has a strong commitment to the principle of supplying systems inclusive of full on-site training and customer support; this ensures that all staff, fee-earners and partners are able to utilise the Quill system to its full potential. In addition, a telephone hot line team is available all day to answer user enquiries. Quill has software to meet the needs of firms of all sizes and the cost-effectiveness of its systems can be demonstrated to even the small and medium-sized practices. Whether starting from scratch or upgrading an existing system, Quill's advice will be appropriate to firms' budgets as well as their current and future needs. All hardware is tested by Quill on their own premises prior to installation and the project team will ensure the smooth transition and implementation of the new system. The product portfolio includes integrated accounting, time recording and case management (which integrate with WordPerfect) for conveyancing, crime, matrimonial, personal injury and uninsured loss, debt collection, mortgage repossession, housing disrepair and general database applications.

QUINTEC INTERNATIONAL LIMITED

Head Office: 11-13 Capricorn Centre, Cranes Farm Road, Basildon, Essex SS14 3JJ

Tel: 01268 270601
Fax: 01268 270602
E-Mail: royr@quintec.co.uk
Helpdesk available
Normal office hours

Contact: Roy Russell, Business Manager

Business established in 192
No. of Directors 4
No. of Staff: 40
Target firm size: Any / All

PRODUCT DETAILS

CompareRite from Lexis-Nexis a division of Reed Elsevier Inc.

Environments Supported
Windows 3.x - Native
Windows 95 - 16 bit

Application
Document Assembly Systems - General Purpose
Document Assembly Systems - Letter Writing
Document Assembly Systems - Will Drafting

Hotdocs from Capsoft Development Corp.

Environments Supported
Windows 3.x - Native
Windows 95 - 16 bit

Application
Document Assembly Systems - General Purpose
Document Assembly Systems - Letter Writing
Document Assembly Systems - Will Drafting

Company Profile

Quintec International, part of The Quintec Group, is the UK's leading value-added distributor of application productivity and integration tools. The Quintec Group was established in 1992 and currently employs over 40 people. The Quintec Group has its own fully equipped education and training centre at its Basildon headquarters and also provides experienced consultancy, on-site customer training, technical support and integration services to VARs and end users. The Quintec Group has built a strong channel of value added resellers and business partners. Quintec is a Microsoft Solutions Provider and Lotus Business Partner and is currently negotiating other alliances to ensure the support of major IT players for its workgroup product strategy. Workgroup computing is now the major growth area in business computing. Deployment is taking place on a growing scale with many diverse organisations becoming fully aware of the time and financial benefits. As the major distributor, Quintec is experiencing strong growth with an increasing number of pilot schemes moving to full implementation. Quintec has document management systems running on over 160 sites with in excess of 17, 000 licenses - importantly, more than half of these sites have over 100 users. Several installations have 400-500 users and the largest site is running around 1, 000 users. See also CMS OPEN and PC DOCS (UK) Limited.

"If you are using a specialist legal supplier, make sure adequate training is included as part of your contract."

RECORD TIMING LIMITED

Head Office: 23-25 Dalston Lane, London E8 3DF

Tel: 0171 431 0997
Fax: 0171 923 1497
E-Mail: dowse_co@geo2.poptel.org.uk

Contact: Bill Parry-Davies, Director Solicitor
Contact: Chister Sol, Director

Business established in 1994
No. of Directors 2
No. of Staff: 2
Target firm size: Small

PRODUCT DETAILS
Record Timing

Environments Supported
Character-Based Terminal Emulation
DOS
Novell
Windows 3.x - CBT Emulation
Windows 95 - 16 bit
Windows NT

Application
Accounting - Accounts & Time Recording
Case Management - Civil Litigation
Case Management - Criminal
Case Management - General Purpose
Case Management - Personal Injury
Document Assembly Systems - General Purpose
Document Assembly Systems - Letter Writing
Information Management - Document Management
Information Management - Know-How
Information Management - Text Retrieval Software
Legal Aid Franchising
Litigation Support - Document Listing Software
Miscellaneous - Other
Office Systems - Database - Clients and Contacts
Office Systems - Database - Marketing and Mailing
Office Systems - Fee Earner Desktop
Office Systems - Time Recording

Company Profile
Record Timing is a comprehensive client/casework database for realtime recording and costing and for casework management. Designed by solicitors, it is sufficiently flexible to meet any requirement and can be easily customised without computer programming skills. It integrates with conventional legal accounts packages and word processors and has both standard reporting and user-assembled reports by easily selected criteria including invoicing.

RESOLUTION SYSTEMS

Head Office: Lombard Business Park, 20-26 Purley Way, Croydon, Surrey CR0 3JP

Tel: 0171 588 7200
Fax: 0171 588 7244
Helpdesk available
Normal office hours

Contact: James Low, Sales Director

Business established in 1989
No. of Directors 5
No. of Staff: 140
Target firm size: Any / All

PRODUCT DETAILS
FirmWare - Practice Management

Environments Supported
Character-Based Terminal Emulation
UNIX
Windows 3.x - CBT Emulation
Windows 3.x - Native
Windows 95 - 32 bit
Windows NT

Application
Accounting - Accounts & Time Recording
Case Management - Civil Litigation
Case Management - Conveyancing
Case Management - Criminal
Case Management - Debt Collection
Case Management - General Purpose
Case Management - Personal Injury
Case Management - Probate
Case Management - Road Traffic Act Claims
Case Management - Uninsured Loss Recovery
Document Assembly Systems - Letter Writing
Document Assembly Systems - Will Drafting
Electronic Publishing - Legal Forms
Electronic Publishing - Legal Text Books
Electronic Publishing - Online Information Services
Electronic Publishing - Other
Electronic Publishing - Precedents
Information Management - Document Management
Information Management - Know-How
Information Management - Library Systems
Miscellaneous - Other
Office Systems - Database - Clients and Contacts
Office Systems - Database - Marketing and Mailing
Office Systems - Desk-top Faxing
Office Systems - E-mail and shared Diary
Office Systems - Fee Earner Desktop

Company Profile

The Resolution Group have a combined turnover of £14M employing 140 people. Resolution Systems Limited is a specialist network systems integrator with experience of implementing large document/image management systems in legal firms. Resolution SQL Limited are the authors of the FirmWare practice management system and have just released their new client/server Windows version running on Windows NT server. FirmWare includes time recording, client/matter accounting and billing as well as sophisticated contact marketing and case management. Resolution are able to deliver this truly integrated practice management system.

RESPONSIVE SYSTEMS LTD

Head Office: 34A Glazbury Road, London W14 9AS

Tel: 0171 602 4107
Fax: 0171 603 2109
Helpdesk available
8.00am - 6.30pm

Contact: Robin Cameron, Product Development Director

Business established in 1991
No. of Directors 2
No. of Staff: 7
Target firm size: Any / All

PRODUCT DETAILS
Kurzweil VOICE and DragonDictate

Application
Office Systems - Voice Recognition Systems

Company Profile
Over the last year or so, voice response has advanced considerably. It is now a simple to use, inexpensive alternative to learning difficult programs and employing typists to duplicate the document you have just spoken. For example, using your word processor no longer means reading several thousand pages from an obliquely written manual, and then learning complicated sequences of key presses. Instead, you can simply say things like "indent paragraph" or "delete line". The manual instantly reduces to about one or two pages of spoken commands. As you are already a natural speaker there is virtually nothing to learn. There is also an important psychological advantage in being able to create, format, edit, and print out documents in one cycle. The system is designed to be easy and, although you can be trained in its use if you wish, many people take to it immediately. You can sit back comfortably, avoiding RSI, backstrain, and eye fatigue, and talk quietly in your normal voice, in a typical office environment, watching the text appear on screen, including your own special words, phrases, standard clauses, or frequently used documents. The system runs a continuous spell-check as you speak, making errors almost impossible. Voice response can be added to your existing desktop or notebook computer, allowing you to create every kind of document with ease, just using everyday language. A 200,000 word system costs £595 exc VAT and we include free phone/fax support.

RWM DATA MANAGEMENT LTD

**Head Office: 11 Hall Quay, Great Yarmouth, Norfolk
NR30 1HP**

Tel: 01493 853350
Fax: 01493 855766
E-Mail: rwm@paston.co.uk
Helpdesk available
8.00am - 5.30pm

Contact: Bill Stolworthy, Managing Director

Business established in 1994
No. of Directors 2
No. of Staff: 4
Target firm size: Any / All

PRODUCT DETAILS
Alphascan

Environments Supported
Windows 3.x - Native
Windows 95 - 16 bit
Windows 95 - 32 bit

Application
Information Management - Document Management
Information Management - Text Retrieval Software
Litigation Support - Image-based Discovery Systems

Company Profile
RWM Data Management Ltd is a bureau providing a
complete imaging service. They do not sell either software
or hardware. Alphascan has been used in several major
litigations, mainly construction based where large amounts
of documentation are normal. No additional software is
required; everything needed is included on the compact
disk. With no capital expenditure, Alphascan runs on
normal PCs with CD-ROMs.

SANDERSON GA LTD

**Head Office: 1-2 Venture Way, Aston Science Park,
Birmingham, West Midlands B7 4AP**

Tel: 0121 359 4861
Fax: 0121 359 3283

Contact: Allan Hodkinson, Sales Director

No. of Directors 6
No. of Staff: 80

PRODUCT DETAILS
QNIX

Environments Supported
Character-Based Terminal Emulation
DOS
UNIX
Windows 3.x - Native

Application
Accounting - Accounts & Time Recording
Case Management - Civil Litigation
Case Management - Conveyancing
Case Management - Criminal
Case Management - Debt Collection
Case Management - General Purpose
Case Management - Mortgage Repossessions
Case Management - Personal Injury
Case Management - Probate
Document Assembly Systems - General Purpose
Document Assembly Systems - Letter Writing
Document Assembly Systems - Will Drafting
Information Management - Document Management
Legal Aid Franchising
Office Systems - Database - Clients and Contacts
Office Systems - Database - Marketing and Mailing

Company Profile
Sanderson GA are a major supplier of computer systems
and application software. As a member of Sanderson
Electronics plc the combined group turnover is in excess of
£50 million. Sanderson GA have been providing software,
hardware and associated services to the legal profession
since 1982 and have been involved in excess of 400
successful installations. The QNIX software includes a
number of closely integrated modules which can be
installed either as part of a fully integrated system or can
stand alone.

SELECT LEGAL SYSTEMS LIMITED

Head Office: Haisell House, 4 Hull Road, Hessle, North Humberside HU13 OAH

Tel: 01482 644 334
Fax: 01482 641 096
Helpdesk available
Normal office hours

Contact: Steve Ness, Sales Director

Business established in 1993
No. of Directors 3
No. of Staff: 7
Target firm size: Any / All

PRODUCT DETAILS
Select Accounts

Environments Supported
Character-Based Terminal Emulation
UNIX
Windows 3.x - CBT Emulation

Application
Accounting - Accounts & Time Recording

Select Case Management

Environments Supported
Character-Based Terminal Emulation
UNIX
Windows 3.x - CBT Emulation

Application
Case Management - Conveyancing
Case Management - Criminal
Case Management - General Purpose
Case Management - Personal Injury

Select Client Database

Environments Supported
Character-Based Terminal Emulation
UNIX
Windows 3.x - CBT Emulation

Application
Office Systems - Database - Clients and Contacts

Select PMS

Environments Supported
Character-Based Terminal Emulation
UNIX
Windows 3.x - CBT Emulation

Application
Accounting - Accounts & Time Recording
Accounting - Accounts (no Time Recording)
Case Management - Conveyancing
Case Management - Criminal
Case Management - General Purpose
Case Management - Personal Injury
Information Management - Document Management
Legal Aid Franchising
Office Systems - Database - Clients and Contacts
Office Systems - Database - Marketing and Mailing
Office Systems - E-mail and shared Diary
Office Systems - Fee Earner Desktop

Select Purchase Ledger

Environments Supported
Character-Based Terminal Emulation
Windows 3.x - CBT Emulation

Application
Accounting - Accounts & Time Recording

Select Time Recording

Environments Supported
Character-Based Terminal Emulation
UNIX
Windows 3.x - CBT Emulation

Application
Office Systems - Time Recording

Company Profile
Select PMS can be implemented as modules in the preferred sequence for the practice. The Client database module is the "core" of the system and is, therefore, a mandatory requirement. All other modules are optional. This ensures a true database is implemented, with client, contact and matter information entered once only and stored in one place on the system.

SOFTWARE SOLUTIONS (UK) LIMITED

Head Office: 340A Shirley Road, Southampton, Hampshire S015 3HT

Tel: 01703 789107
Fax: 01703 701978
Helpdesk available
Normal office hours

Contact: Mike Evans, Sales Director

Business established in 1989
No. of Directors 3
No. of Staff: 14
Target firm size: Any / All

PRODUCT DETAILS
CoAct Company Secretarial Software

Environments Supported
Windows 3.x - Native
Windows 95 - 32 bit

Application
Document Assembly Systems - General Purpose
Electronic Publishing - Legal Forms

Company Profile
CoAct performs all levels of company secretarial work. The software produces approved Companies House Forms, Minutes, Notices, Resolutions and other related documents. There is an extensive technical guideline section. A validate option ensures that companies have all of the required information recorded for them. An extensive compliance diary ensures that all work is performed on time, with extensive planning and reporting options. The latest release offers a billing module, automatic links to external word processors and an Incorporation module. We now have over 600 users of our system with many being solicitors in practice.

SOLACE LEGAL SYSTEMS

Head Office: Bank House, 65 High Street, Stamford, Lincolnshire PE9 2AW

Tel: 01780 64947
Fax: 01780 66073
E-Mail: sales@stukeley.demon.co.uk
Helpdesk available
Normal office hours

Contact: Gerard Barden, Sales and Marketing Manager

Business established in 1981
No. of Staff: 14
Target firm size: Any/All

PRODUCT DETAILS
Solace Accounting & Time Recording

Environments Supported
Character-Based Terminal Emulation
DOS
UNIX
Windows 3.x - Native
Windows 95 - 16 bit
Windows 95 - 32 bit
Windows NT

Application
Accounting - Accounts & Time Recording
Accounting - Accounts (no Time Recording).

Solcase

Environments Supported
Character-Based Terminal Emulation
Novell
UNIX
Windows 3.x - CBT Emulation
Windows 3.x - Native
Windows 95 - 16 bit
Windows 95 - 32 bit
Windows NT

Application
Case Management - Conveyancing
Case Management - Debt Collection
Case Management - General Purpose
Case Management - Personal Injury
Document Assembly Systems - General Purpose
Electronic Publishing - Legal Forms
Information Management - Document Management
Office Systems - Database - Clients and Contacts
Office Systems - Database - Marketing and Mailing
Office Systems - Desk-top Faxing
Office Systems - E-mail and shared Diary

Company Profile

With over 350 installations, the Solace range of modular applications have been consistently delivering performance, reliability and security for the legal profession since 1981. The availability of new Windows desktop tools (Time Recording II and Matter Enquiry), a powerful Legal Aid Tracking database and our cost effective Debt Recovery system combine with our established applications, to form an integrated portfolio of products for practices of all sizes. In addition, we offer a full hardware and systems consultancy service including local and wide area networks, client/server, ISDN communication, data storage and system migration, as we continue to work towards a total solution for the legal office.

SOLICITORS OWN SOFTWARE

Head Office: 2 Brock Street, Bath, Avon BA1 2LN

Tel: 01225 448664
Fax: 01225 480057
Helpdesk available
Normal office hours

Contact: David McNamara, Sales Director

Business established in 1987
No. of Directors 3
No. of Staff: 11
Target firm size: Small, Medium

PRODUCT DETAILS
SOS Case Manager

Environments Supported
Novell
Windows 3.x - Native
Windows 95 - 16 bit
Windows 95 - 32 bit
Windows NT

Application
Case Management - Conveyancing
Case Management - Debt Collection
Case Management - General Purpose
Case Management - Personal Injury
Case Management - Uninsured Loss Recovery
Information Management - Document Management

SOS Practice Manager Accounts

Environments Supported
Novell
Windows 3.x - Native
Windows 95 - 16 bit
Windows 95 - 32 bit
Windows NT

Application
Accounting - Accounts & Time Recording
Accounting - Accounts (no Time Recording)
Office Systems - Database - Clients and Contacts
Office Systems - Fee Earner Desktop

SOS Probate Manager

Environments Supported
Novell
Windows 3.x - Native
Windows 95 - 16 bit
Windows 95 - 32 bit
Windows NT

Application
Case Management - Probate

SOS Time Manager

Environments Supported
Novell
Windows 3.x - Native
Windows 95 - 16 bit
Windows 95 - 32 bit
Windows NT

Application
Office Systems - Time Recording

Company Profile
SOS are one of the first companies to offer a fully
integrated range of "true Windows" designed software.
Modules available include accounts, time recording, case
management and document management, in fact everything
needed to create an entire "practice-wide" system. Once
details of a new file have been entered, a fee-earner can
record time, view ledgers, generate documents
automatically and produce bills, all achieved by simply
"pointing" with the mouse on the screen. All SOS software
modules can be used independently, enabling a practice to
start with one module and expand gradually at a pace to
suit the practice.

SOPHCO SYSTEMS LIMITED

**Head Office: 3 Ransomes Mews, Great Eastern Wharf,
Parkgate Road, London SW11 4NP**

Tel: 0171 924 4124
Fax: 0171 924 2959
Helpdesk available
Normal office hours

Contact: Audrey Errington, Product Manager
Contact: Brian Smith, Managing Director

Business established in 1979
No. of Directors 3
No. of Staff: 14
Target firm size: Medium, Large

PRODUCT DETAILS
Legacase - Case Management

Environments Supported
Character-Based Terminal Emulation
DOS
Novell
UNIX
Windows 3.x - CBT Emulation

Application
Case Management - Civil Litigation
Case Management - Conveyancing
Case Management - Criminal
Case Management - Debt Collection
Case Management - General Purpose
Case Management - Personal Injury
Case Management - Probate
Case Management - Road Traffic Act Claims
Case Management - Uninsured Loss Recovery
Document Assembly Systems - General Purpose
Document Assembly Systems - Letter Writing
Document Assembly Systems - Will Drafting
Electronic Publishing - Legal Forms

Legasys - Accounting

Environments Supported
Character-Based Terminal Emulation
DOS
Novell
UNIX
Windows 3.x - CBT Emulation

Application
Accounting - Accounts (no Time Recording)
Office Systems - Database - Clients and Contacts
Office Systems - Database - Marketing and Mailing
Office Systems - Desk-top Faxing
Office Systems - E-mail and shared Diary
Office Systems - Fee Earner Desktop

Legatime - Time Recording

Environments Supported
Character-Based Terminal Emulation
DOS
Novell
UNIX
Windows 3.x - CBT Emulation

Application
Accounting - Accounts & Time Recording
Office Systems - Time Recording

Company Profile
We provide integrated office automation systems for the
legal profession. We offer both hardware and software with
full training and on-going support. Established in 1979 we
are committed to the support and development of all our
products and services for the legal office.

SPD LIMITED

**Head Office: 2A Mansfield Business Park, Lymington
Bottom Road, Four Marks, Alton, Hampshire GU34 5PZ**

Tel: 01420 563588
Fax: 01420 562206
Helpdesk available
Normal office hours

Contact: John Roy, Head of Systems Group

Business established in 1988
No. of Directors 1
No. of Staff: 12
Target firm size: Any / All

PRODUCT DETAILS
Voice - IBM VoiceType Speech Software

Environments Supported
Windows 3.x - Native
Windows 95 - 16 bit

Application
Office Systems - Voice Recognition Systems

Company Profile
We are a well established supplier of PC systems,
assembled to order mainly for trade customers and
resellers. We are also agents for IBM VoiceType speech
dictation systems, offering a complete voice operated
solution including a quality Pentium PC, business software
and IBM VoiceType, with full installation, training and
support.

SYSTEM ONE

Head Office: Lavant House, 39 Lavant Street, Petersfield, Hampshire GU34 1JS

Tel: 01730 267000
Fax: 01730 266676
Helpdesk available
Normal office hours

Contact: Jonathan Caines

Business established in 1982
No. of Directors 2
Target firm size: Small, Medium

PRODUCT DETAILS
NOMOS

Environments Supported
DOS

Application
Accounting - Accounts & Time Recording
Accounting - Accounts (no Time Recording)

Company Profile

NOMOS Accounts and Time Recording package is designed for the small to medium sized practice running on DOS based IBM compatible machines. The system was designed by a practising London solicitor, therefore all information is displayed in a familiar form. SYSTEM ONE has been established since 1982 and in this time we have sold NOMOS to well over 100 practising solicitors as well as several bureaux. Single user price £1250.00.

TAXSOFT LTD

Head Office: Addington House, 5 Compton Road, London SW19 7QA

Tel: 0181 296 1400
Fax: 0181 296 1499
Helpdesk available
Normal office hours

Contact: Fiona Tytler, Business Services Manager

Business established in 1983
No. of Directors 5
No. of Staff: 70
Target firm size: Any / All

PRODUCT DETAILS
Personal Tax For Windows

Environments Supported
Windows 3.x - Native
Windows 95 - 16 bit
Windows NT

Application
Financial Services - Personal Tax Returns
Financial Services - Tax Planning
Other

Company Profile

The leading supplier of taxation software, established in 1983, Taxsoft has remained in the same ownership throughout its history. Its products are used by professional practices (including 7 of the top 10 firms of accountants) and by many industrial companies. Personal Tax, Business Tax (Self Assessment), Corporation Tax (including Pay and File), Group Tax Planning, Deferred Tax and Tax Administration.

TEXTSTORE LIMITED

**Head Office: PO Box 87, Horsham, West Sussex
RH13 7YD**

Tel: 01403 257348
Fax: 01403 257348
Helpdesk available
Normal office hours (0860 709107)

Contact: Paul Ashley, Managing Director

Business established in 1982
No. of Directors 1
No. of Staff: 3

PRODUCT DETAILS
Conveyancing Assistant

Environments Supported
DOS
Novell
Windows 3.x - CBT Emulation
Windows NT

Application
Case Management - Conveyancing

Probate Assistant

Environments Supported
DOS
Novell
Windows 3.x - CBT Emulation
Windows NT

Application
Case Management - Probate

Solledger

Environments Supported
DOS
Novell
Windows 3.x - CBT Emulation
Windows NT

Application
Accounting - Accounts & Time Recording
Accounting - Accounts (no Time Recording)
Accounting - Estate Accounts
Accounting - Trust Accounts

Company Profile

Textstore Limited was established in 1982 to take over the business of Lewis Ashley computers who had developed accounts programs from the earlier days of micro computers using their strong accounting background to great advantage. Solledger, our legal accounting and time recording software, was launched in 1982 and has been continually developed and improved since then. The company is very close to the 140 users of Solledger and prides itself on the level of service it can give and the very competitive cost of its products and services. The company has always supplied hardware where required and lately has increasingly become involved in projects to supply networks of computers to legal firms with a terminal on every desk. Shortly to be launched are three new case management programs covering conveyancing, probate and trust work.

THE BEAVER CORPORATION

Head Office: Temple Chambers, Temple Avenue, London EC4Y 0HP

Tel: 0171 936 2828
Fax: 0171 583 1531

Contact: Michael Wiilstrop, Managing Director

Business established in 1987
No. of Directors 3
No. of Staff: 10
Target firm size: Any / All

PRODUCT DETAILS
Legal Arms

Environments Supported
DOS
Novell
UNIX
Windows 3.x - Native
Windows 95 - 32 bit
Windows NT

Application
Case Management - Debt Collection

Property Arms

Environments Supported
DOS
Novell
UNIX
Windows 3.x - Native
Windows 95 - 32 bit
Windows NT

Application
Case Management - Debt Collection
Case Management - Landlord & Tenant
Case Management - Mortgage Repossessions

Company Profile

Since the launch of Beaver's ARMS pre-legal and legal "cradle-to-grave" debt recovery packages in 1990, Beaver has grown to become one of the most respected specialist suppliers in the business. Beaver's debt recovery products are installed in over 300 organisations. These include over 100 law firms as well as many major corporates, debt recovery agencies and local authorities. ARMS products are available in DOS and UNIX, and 1996 sees the launch of Beaver's Windows NT versions, including the introduction of SQL client/server for high volume processing. Beaver are active members of the Civil Court Users Association and the High Court Users Association, and are recognised by the LCD, ensuring products and services reflect the very latest changes in legislation and that the highest quality standards are maintained. Beaver is renowned for achieving integration with a large number of third party accounting systems, allowing users to select debt recovery software on its own merits, whilst at the same time ensuring a total, integrated solution is achieved. ARMS products are distributed to local authorities exclusively by Radius plc - telephone 0181 844 2141. Locations at Feltham, Watford, Milton Keynes, Leicester, Leeds, Dronfield, Darlaston, Cardiff, Hull and Edinburgh.

❝The existence of an up to date business plan is crucial to the IT decision.❞

Thompson Moore Associates Ltd

Head Office: Windlesham Court, 53 Guildford Road, Bagshot, Surrey GU19 5NG

Tel: 01276 452070
Fax: 01276 451589
E-Mail: post@tma-sims.demon.co.uk

Contact: Peter Moore, Director

Product Details
SiMS - Solicitors Integrated Management System

Application
Accounting - Accounts & Time Recording
Office Systems - Database - Clients and Contacts
Office Systems - Database - Marketing and Mailing
Office Systems - Quality Management/Client Care Steps
Office Systems - Time Recording

Company Profile
Thompson Moore have been supporting the legal profession since 1984, during which time the specialist legal and system development background of our staff have enabled close working partnerships with our clients. These clients are mainly within the medium to large sized firms requiring tailored IT solutions to maintain their own competitive edge. The Solicitors Integrated Management System (SiMS) is a totally integrated practice management system, written from first principles using Progress 4GL and Relational Database. The application centres around a Registry and Marketing core which focuses on assisting the practice develop the business relationship with clients and potential clients. Integrated with this core are the financial accounting and time recording elements. Emphasis has been placed on performance reporting at all levels within the firm as well as assisting with tight fiscal control. Full advantage can be taken of the powerful 4GL Query facilities, the links to spreadsheet and word processing systems and a truly "Open Systems" approach to the most cost effective solution.

Timeslice Ltd

Head Office: William Gaitskell House, 23 Paradise Street, Rotherhithe, London SE16 4QD

Tel: 0171 231 0073
Fax: 0171 237 9806

Contact: Brendan Conroy, Marketing Manager

No. of Directors 3

Product Details
ACTIONMAN

Environments Supported
Character-Based Terminal Emulation
Novell
UNIX
Windows 3.x - CBT Emulation
Windows 3.x - Native
Windows 95 - 16 bit
Windows 95 - 32 bit
Windows NT

Application
Case Management - Conveyancing
Case Management - Debt Collection
Case Management - Uninsured Loss Recovery

LawMan

Environments Supported
Character-Based Terminal Emulation
Novell
UNIX
Windows 3.x - CBT Emulation
Windows 3.x - Native
Windows 95 - 16 bit
Windows 95 - 32 bit
Windows NT

Application
Accounting - Accounts & Time Recording
Accounting - Accounts (no Time Recording)
Legal Aid Franchising
Litigation Support - Document Listing Software
Miscellaneous - Other
Office Systems - Database - Clients and Contacts
Office Systems - Database - Marketing and Mailing
Office Systems - Desk-top Faxing
Office Systems - E-mail and shared Diary
Office Systems - Fee Earner Desktop

Company Profile

TIMESLICE is an ISO 9001 and Tick-IT accredited company, with a long established presence in the legal marketplace. Timeslice systems are designed to be backwards compatible and flexible, allowing customers to upgrade their systems modularly, while guaranteeing seamless integration between system components and several third party products, e.g. Carpe Diem. Product flexibilty is further illustrated by the way both "LawMan for Windows" and "DebtManager for Windows" allow the system to operate either in a Windows environment or via ASCII terminal emulation: this helps to preserve customers' investment in existing equipment. All systems provide intuitive access and "drill-down" facilities for ease of operation. LawMan is a comprehensive practice management and legal accounting system, with additional modules for Legal Aid, Archives and Deeds, and Marketing. The ACTIONMAN group of products are event driven workflow/legal support systems. These are extremely flexible and allow users to modify systems to match both their own and an individual client's requirements. The group comprises: DebtManager - Debt collection from pre-litigation through to enforcement; Conveyancer - Conveyancing; and LitigationManager - Uninsured Loss Recovery and Insurance Litigation.

TOTAL COMPUTER SYSTEMS

Head Office: 117 High Street, Epping, Essex CM16 4BD

Tel: 01992 575151
Fax: 01992 575147
E-Mail: Total@comp.netconect.co.uk
Helpdesk available
Normal office hours

Contact: Tony Westray

Business established in 1988
No. of Directors 2
No. of Staff: 18
Target firm size: Medium

PRODUCT DETAILS
Openfile

Environments Supported
Novell
UNIX
Windows 3.x - Native
Windows 95 - 16 bit
Windows 95 - 32 bit
Windows NT

Application
Case Management - Civil Litigation
Case Management - Conveyancing
Case Management - Criminal
Case Management - General Purpose
Case Management - Personal Injury
Case Management - Road Traffic Act Claims
Case Management - Uninsured Loss Recovery
Document Assembly Systems - General Purpose
Document Assembly Systems - Letter Writing
Document Assembly Systems - Will Drafting
Information Management - Document Management
Information Management - Know-How
Information Management - Library Systems
Information Management - Text Retrieval Software
Legal Aid Franchising
Litigation Support - Document Listing Software
Litigation Support - Image-based Discovery Systems
Office Systems - Database - Clients and Contacts
Office Systems - Database - Marketing and Mailing
Office Systems - Desk-top Faxing
Office Systems - E-mail and shared Diary
Office Systems - Fee Earner Desktop

Company Profile

Total Computer Systems (TCS) is a UK software services company specialising within commercial, local government, central government and legal markets. We develop systems to ensure that primary data is used both efficiently and productively by producing applications that incorporate groupware and workflow products. Our company objective is to supply systems and services that increase team and personal productivity. TCS also develops software for hand-held computing devices, that interface with the above and/or existing core corporate information systems, to ensure that end-user data is captured both accurately and efficiently and delivered in an easy to use form. Our skill areas are as follows: Groupware & procedure based processing systems using LOTUS Notes in a Windows PC environment as well as UNIX and OS/2; Hand held PC or Pen-based software development for data storage, collection and retrieval; Hand held PC integration into both Local and Wide Area Networks whether in an Open System or proprietary environment; Communications expertise in Local and Wide Area Networking. The services offered in the delivery of these products are: Application Analysis, Design, Development and Implementation; Training; Software and Systems Support; Consultancy.

VIDESS LTD

Head Office: 633 Halifax Road, Liversedge, West Yorkshire WF15 8HG

Tel: 01274 851577
Fax: 01274 851631
Helpdesk available
Normal office hours

Contact: C. Rose, Sales Director
Contact: P.D. Sanderson, Managing Director

Business established in 1977
No. of Directors 3
No. of Staff: 25
Target firm size: Any / All

PRODUCT DETAILS
Case Conveyancing

Environments Supported
Character-Based Terminal Emulation
DOS
Novell
UNIX
VAX/VMS
Windows 3.x - CBT Emulation
Windows 3.x - Native
Windows 95 - 16 bit
Windows 95 - 32 bit
Windows NT

Case Conveyancing

Application
Case Management - Conveyancing

Case Criminal

Application
Case Management - Criminal

Case Debt Collection

Application
Case Management - Debt Collection

Case Mortgage Repossession

Application
Case Management - Mortgage Repossessions

Case Properties In Possession

Application
Case Management - Mortgage Repossessions

Case Remortgage

Application
Case Management - Conveyancing

Case Toolkit

Application
Case Management - General Purpose

Central Database

Application
Office Systems - Database - Clients and Contacts
Office Systems - Database - Marketing and Mailing

Child Ledger

Application
Calculators - Child Support Act

Client Ledger

Application
Accounting - Accounts & Time Recording

Expertease

Application
Information Management - Document Management
Information Management - Know-How

Fortis Ledger

Application
Miscellaneous - Other

Nominal Ledger

Application
Accounting - Accounts & Time Recording

Organiser

Application
Office Systems - E-mail and shared Diary
Office Systems - Fee Earner Desktop

Pay Ledger

Application
Miscellaneous - Other

Purchase Ledger

Application
Accounting - Accounts & Time Recording

Time Ledger

Application
Legal Aid Franchising
Office Systems - E-mail and shared Diary
Office Systems - Fee Earner Desktop
Office Systems - Time Recording

Company Profile
Established in 1977, Videss has become one of the country's leading suppliers of integrated systems to the legal profession. The unique software developed by Videss and known as the Videss Legal Office is an integrated information collection, storage, retrieval, processing and distribution system developed from the ground up as a "do anything, anywhere, anytime" suite of software. To be technical, it is a "state of the art", 32 bit, 4GL, RDBMS, client-server, ODBC, Character or GUI suite of Open Systems "Progress" application software that provides "Front Office" productivity tools which are fully integrated with "Back Office" procedures. To be practical, it is software that enables fee-earners to produce more accurate work, with less effort, in less time, with fewer staff, for less cost. The Videss Legal Office includes a client database, accounts, time costing, billing (including a legal aid billing, form filling and payment system). System-wide features include Address Lists, Action Lists, Diary, Planner, ToDo Lists, Telephone messages and E-mail system. A wide range of event driven Case Management applications are available all featuring user definable databases constructed using a Windows point, click, drag and drop tool kit. Case applications are fully integrated with other applications and also integrate with Word, WordPerfect and WordPro word processors.

FACTSHEETS INTRODUCTION

These factsheets are designed to help lawyers in private practice with the preliminary stages leading up to the purchase of any new case management or support software for their practices. There are sections dealing with particular features and issues concerning the types of practice support in widespread use today:

- Practice support systems
- Specific practice support, Wills, Document logging and Marketing
- Accounts
- General purpose case management
- Specific types of case management, Debt recovery, Conveyancing and Probate

Please note that wider issues of computer systems in the working legal practice are discussed in the "Practice support systems" section, while more application-specific questions are addressed in the relevant sections. Equally, wider issues of case management, also concerning Conveyancing, Debt collection and Probate are covered in the general section, while matters specific to Conveyancing, Debt recovery or Probate are in those sections. Accounts questions will also apply in some cases to Trust and Wills matters. Therefore it is important that you read the factsheets with this in mind. As you read you may like to compile a list of questions for prospective suppliers. Those questions will grow more detailed as you read through to the more specific sections.

These factsheets provide a list of points which should be borne in mind when deciding what features will be required by your particular practice. While no such list can be exhaustive, some features will not apply to your situation or needs. For instance, features such as integration with other computerised packages will not be necessary for the sole practitioner looking for a stand alone case management system. It would be relevant if the firm was planning that its installation would enable future expansion and have more comprehensive automation of office procedures.

Planning for a new system

The decision to install for the first time or renew a computer system should be taken with great care.

Even before doing the detailed planning, think about longer term planning (look ahead to five years' time). Have you considered what you will need in five years' time and how that affects your immediate needs? Many firms do not have a clear understanding of what legal work they hope/expect to be doing in five years' time and how they should deliver their services then. Although a review of the way a firm is likely to be developed in the near future can help lead to products that meet the firm's immediate needs, some argue that selecting the supplier with the right long term strategy may be more important than product in the medium term as suppliers should be more constant than their products. This approach puts greater emphasis on the strategy and longer term supplier appraisal than on mere selection and implementation of a system.

Just as in the planning of any new investment, a coherent and properly supported plan should be formed within your firm. Firm size is important when choosing a system. If you are a sole practitioner, the level of analysis and the degree of expertise required to solve your administrative problems will not be the same as for the firm with several partners and numerous staff in various departments. Some firms may feel the need for professional advice. What is similar for all is that a system that in some way does not do its job will cause considerable difficulty.

Therefore the management of this potential upheaval must be careful, detailed and supported throughout the firm. Be clear what systems need to be modernised, and to what extent; where to find the money; how to find the time. Justification should be made as to cost and competition aspects. Proper interviews should be held with suppliers, other users and prospective users within your firm.

The system must be able to cope with the throughput you require of it for some time in the future. What are your projections? It must be usable. This will vary with the size of firm, while a large system may be fairly complex, a smaller one may be simpler to manage using the "jack-of-all-trades" approach required of the small business.

The usability also depends on the capabilities of the prospective users. Those users may include fee-earners and partners. However competent the users may be, they require proper and adequate training, which must be designed around their needs, not left to contingency planning. Time and money must be set aside. Remember that, for all the stories of computer glitches and poor software, very often the loss of data or calls for support to the supplier will be due to the user's lack of training. When considering who should be trained, think also of the illness and holiday replacements who must not only be trained but kept up to date regularly as well. Training will also ease the introduction of the new system.

Remember that as with any physical system, there is the upkeep and maintenance to bear in mind. There are two functions of a system: day-to-day use and the administrative level. During the introduction of the system, adjustments will be needed to both functions, to the way the system works and the way the users work. Does your firm require a full-time administrator for management, trouble-shooting and upkeep of the system, or will close support by the supplier during introduction followed by regular housekeeping afterwards suffice? Who will do that housekeeping?

Questions to ask yourself about the way you work

Most practice support systems require a degree of adaptation of working methods by their users, if only that the matter details have to be input on the computer keyboard. Some systems need feeding regularly with lots of data input (details of the day's post etc.) which may require a change to the daily routine. Some offer to tell the user what to do next. Others wait to be told what to do.

The style or approach of a software package will influence its suitability for your present style or approach to work. Your present system of document production, diary reminders and "to do" lists may be fully or partially automatic, or comprise partially or entirely personal systems, such as individually dictated letters and desk diaries. Consider this aspect very carefully, as many users find it difficult, for instance, to relinquish their desk diaries and participate fully in the shared electronic version.

Ask yourself:

- What do you want the system to achieve?
- To what extent are you and your firm prepared to adapt?
- Do you want to delegate more to secretaries and junior staff? How will the system help you do this?
- How much does each fee-earner want to use the system? Does it rely on everyone joining in fully (e.g. electronic diaries)?
- Are you prepared to put someone in charge of managing the system?
- Do you want the system to produce documents and forms?
- Do you want a procedural-based approach?
- Do you want to drive it, have it prompt you, or let it run automatically?
- Do you want to use preset case procedure designs (if not, check how easily you can change or over-ride them - will you need expensive programming help to add a new letter or extra step - will you have to go to your supplier for this)?
- Will you use the supplier's standard letters (if not, check how easily you can change or override them - will you need expensive programming help - will you have to go to your supplier for this)?

ACCOUNTING AND TIME RECORDING PACKAGES

Most legal accounts and time recording systems were developed initially as cashier-based systems. Increasingly, the features expected of modern management accounts have been added. It is now very unusual to find a new system that cannot print out a full management reporting pack and exception reports directly from the system, that does not report on aged creditors and debtors, offer a spreadsheet interface for those wanting to use a PC spreadsheet and offer detailed work in progress analysis and reports.

Legal accounts were traditionally seen as being different from those of other businesses. Many now question this, especially in the light of recent encroachment on solicitors' traditional markets and competition from other professions and businesses. There can be many benefits from having a generic accounting package adjusted to fit your practice, not the least being the larger investment in development and the dedicated accounting support.

PACKAGE-SPECIFIC ISSUES

The list of issues below concern the day-to-day operation, use and productivity of accounting and time recording packages. You should consider, in consultation with the eventual users, the relevance and importance of all of these to your firm when putting together your requirements. Then you can decide which of the packages on offer will best suit your firm.

Note that the whole question of trying to evaluate an accounting package on the basis of a demonstration and test is so complex as to be, in the opinion of some, almost impossible, whatever time is available. There is no substitute for a visit to a comparable firm where the package has had time to settle down and the person responsible can give a reasonably informed, and objective, view of its performance and capabilities.

Configuration

Multiple bank account reconciliation

Where the package enables you to keep a user-defined number of accounts open at any time with online reconciliation of each one.

Multiple branch

Accounts for more than one branch can be run from a central system. Ensure that the accounts coding allows analysis in any permutation of the branch code so that detailed branch office reporting and analysis of individual branch and aggregate firm figures is possible.

Multi-currency

Accounting for investments, purchases and disbursements in other currencies.

Asset register

Probably a luxury for most firms. Should keep full asset details with facilities for varying rates of depreciation, and detailed printout reports for annual accounts.

Period-based: closure of periods possible

After final reconciliations and write-offs, individual periods may be finalised and denied update.

Multiple open years / periods

Ability to have unresolved periods open at the same time for postings or multiple balances forward, e.g. starting the new financial year while still waiting for postings to the last one.

This ability to keep one period open while processing the next one(s) is critical (and rarely available in solicitor's accounting packages).

Automatic prepayments and accruals

You may need automatic re-posting of periodic payments, e.g. standing orders and direct debits. Would you prefer a prompt each year or month?

Reports

Can all information be seen on screen and printed? How?

Ability to see a report on screen before printing is very important. Many reports are generated to look at one or two figures so printing is often not necessary.

Client account

Enables compliance with Solicitors Accounts Rules and Deposit Interest Rules

Note that some paper systems enable compliance; key issue is whether system supplies the information needed to act in accordance with the Rules and whether in-house procedures ensure compliance.

General compliance is always up to the operator and internal procedures and the system should not be relied on exclusively.

Compliance with practice quality standards

Do procedures, logic and record keeping comply with quality assurance guidelines, e.g. Law Society, ISO 9000, BS 5750?

Account reconciliation

Ability to reconcile bank and other accounts (e.g. credit card charges).

Prevention of overdrawing

Prevention of overdrawing is in itself of no use as the sequence in which transactions are posted may mean that accounts are frequently overdrawn during a day's postings, particularly on busy accounts such as property conveyancing. However, many systems offer warnings. Check what messages and overrides are used and understand when they occur.

Notional or designated Deposit Account Interest calculation

Calculation of interest on divisions of larger deposits / as a sum of a portfolio of investments. Actual interest / interest due according to guidelines.

Are there sufficient bands and rates for your purposes?

Can the calculations be made at any time on a single matter or a group of matters and at client level?

It should be possible to edit interest calculations and to hold multiple historic rate tables. Also, client account entry should show both entry and clearance dates (latter may default but should be possible to edit).

Trust accounts

These are usually a subject in their own right and should be investigated separately.

Budgets

Budgets

Budgets are often better handled/prepared through a spreadsheet with any data necessary loaded in from or to the accounts system.

Can budgets be set manually / by percentage / formula / copy / split?

Budget variance reports

Automatic / prompted / manual report production compared by month / year to date with budget / previous year(s).

Variance reporting is often handled better through a spreadsheet when the pre-determined reports in the accounts system are inflexible.

Projections

For 'what if' portrayal according to conditions, for forward planning.

These are best handled through spreadsheets (hence the importance of a good, easy to use, link).

Report generator

Flexible reporting

There should be a flexible report generator which permits reports on any permutation of accounts codes and periods, particularly for trial balances.

Financial reports

Profit and loss account

By firm, office, department, work type etc.

Cash flow statements

For efficient allocation of resources.

Links to diary packages may be useful to help timetable critical payments.

Balance sheet

Production of full balance sheet and, where the quality of the underlying accounting makes it useful, full supporting schedules.

Accounting reports

Trial balance

- Journal listings
- Audit trail
- Cash book analysis (likely to be rarely used)

Analysis of timesheet data

Management reports

Monthly management account pack

Work in progress report

Head of department and fee-earner reports

Billing reports - see below

EIS

Some form of flexible Executive Information System would be useful as the reporting pack that is useful today is often redundant tomorrow.

Report generator for ad hoc reports

Flexible reporting

This is very important as "pre-supplied" reports are often of limited value except for training and very small firms.

There should be a flexible report generator which permits reports on any permutation of accounts codes and periods, particularly for trial balances.

Comparisons

Client or parent client / fee-earner / year / department, as required.

By branch or consolidated

As well as other report conditions, this may be useful.

Batch reports

Automatic generation of certain groups may be useful, e.g. circulation to all partners of month-end figures prior to meetings.

Exception reports

User-defined

Can exception report designs be changed by the user (according to user security access)?

What level of skill is required?

The language involved must be fairly comprehensible, or the normal user will be unable to reconfigure procedures that have evolved.

Pre-supplied

What reports are automatically supplied with the package?

Make sure that report providers and users evaluate what is on offer.

VAT

VAT reports in VAT form format and on correct basis

Automatic calculation of VAT on cash or accrual basis.

Automatic generation of returns in the correct format for Customs and Excise detailed and summary reports.

Multiple VAT rates: as the Chancellor often says, nothing is ruled in or out!

VAT posting

Must be possible to post direct to VAT ledger from cash or journal entry.

VAT on inputs

Disbursements should not retain a VAT input coding until they form part of the output bill as attempts by many systems to track VAT in this way often make bill reversal and credit difficult or impossible.

Memo items

Memos in journals

Is it possible to add memos to journal items for your "aides memoires"?

Can you set a flag that will show up on enquiry to show which memo items exist?

Can separate memo entries be made?

Ledgers

Multiple ledgers

Allows multiple ledgers for different types of account or branches?

What consolidation reporting and analysis facilities are there?

Replication of manual ledger card

For visual familiarity, a data entry form that looks like the manual version.

Does it hold running client and office balances for a matter?

Automatic double entry

Make sure this is the configuration, as it is an important safeguard in the way the underlying entries to the system are made.

Other controls are equally if not more important as many reports are built up from one half of the entries - e.g. will the system confirm that the detailed client account balances agree with the nominal ledger total as a regular routine?

Office and client

The facilities and information that can be recorded in client's matter accounts are critical e.g.:

- Adequate treatment of unpaid experts' fees so as to be able to achieve easily compliance with Solicitors Accounts Rules
- Links with time recording
- References on matched items
- References to batches, cheques, transfers etc.
- Should be possible to view transactions in reverse order
- Are they shown on a single screen, with running balances?
- Can accounts, clients and matters be looked up by name and reference number?
- Can you get a quick look-up of billing details?

Integration

- With purchase ledger
- With client / matter records
- With time records
- With all other accounting records
- With payroll for staff costs

Nominal accounts

Full user-defined nominal ledger system will allow you to replicate your own nominal system.

It is useful to be able to restrict or prohibit direct posting to specified accounts e.g. control accounts.

Stakeholder ledger

It is useful to be able to associate several levels of account other than office or client accounts with individual matters.

Automatic apportionment of invoices / remittances

E.g. to fee-earners, cost / profit centres, areas of activity. But it must be possible to override or edit this.

Purchase

Invoice breakdown

Drill-down access to details and individual items is useful.

Remittance advice production

This should be fully configurable.

Also should be possible to do BACS output and cheque printing facility using one of your firm's standard templates for continuity and convenience.

Settlement discount diary

Take advantage of discounts offered by suppliers / manage cash flow by logical use of diary dates (possibly a luxury).

Integration

- With matter ledgers for disbursements
- Treatment of Counsel's fees
- Automatic reminders of items to be paid

Journals

Can you design your own data entry screens or journals?

Journals to reverse incorrect postings

Full journal analysis, audit trail and reporting

Double entry system

All journals part of the double entry system, and updated together.

BILLING
Sales & fees

Cash basis or bills rendered basis

Alternative basis permissible for reports, clients.

Bill posting routines are very important and poor facilities can take up excess operator time.

Extensive use should be made of default procedures (e.g. assuming that all disbursements will be billed).

Procedures must identify the distinction between disbursements for the Solicitors Accounts Rules and expenses and disbursements for the VAT rules.

Allocation of profit costs / posting of bills
What options are offered?

Bill reversal and credit procedures
These should be straightforward, particularly if the bill has already been paid.

Billing data

Integration with accounting
For seamless reporting / data manipulation, e.g. by fee-earner/profit centre / activity area / activity type.

System should distinguish client billed (i.e. to whom the service is provided) from party/parties due to pay the bill.

Rates
- By cost / charge out / legal aid scale
- Rates for different status fee-earners; ability to apply different status rates to one individual fee-earner
- Overtime / ad hoc / client related / normal rates
- Rates for different courts / different status

Postings
By time / activity / non-chargeable (activity defined?)

Bill production
- Manual
- Prompted with manual bill make-up
- Prompted with automatic bill make-up
- Direct, automatic transfer from case management system
- Fixed fee option

Billing guides
- Automatic / manual quotation
- Client oriented billing guides
- Client group billing
- Automatic inclusion of disbursements

- Adding anticipated time
- Writing off time
- Revaluing time

Billing frequency
- Interim / final only / to period
- Automatic / prompted / manual

Payments
- Money on account / instalments dealt with
- User can adjust or override
- E.g. reversing / cancelling bills

Billing reports
Billing enquiries

Flexible reporting by client or matter

Client / Client group reports

Bill production
- Draft bill
- Detailed billing option: provision of itemised bills with no extra work
- Split third party bills

Outstanding bill details

Timely billing reminders

Credit limits
Client / matter / Green Form.

Reminder letters
- Automatic / prompted / manual
- Control by accounts / fee-earner
- Links to word processing packages

Disbursements

Fee-earner / department
Budgets and performance shown against various criteria.

Billing profit success
Profitability by client / matter / overall / fee earner easily and quickly displayed.

Slow moving matters

Work in progress
- Automatically / prompted / manually initiated calculation
- Billed / unbilled
- Paid / unpaid

Aged work in progress calculations
Automatic / periodic / manual.

Written off work in progress recorded

Sophisticated enquiry facility enabling user to generate own reports

Credit control
Parameters
Links to party due to pay as well as party actually billed (client).

Such as definable credit controls for each client, optional interest on unpaid bills.

Reminders
Automatic / prompted / manual generation.

Links to word processing packages.

Ability to produce periodic statements by clients.

Aged creditors report
Automatic / by amount / overdue period.

Advice given to all responsible partners prior to proposed action?

TIME RECORDING
Time control
Time
Clock-based recording/against user-defined activity codes.

On-screen timing whilst using a screen.

Some packages include automatic phone dialling and call duration.

Ideally, time recording should link to case management and be able to record all information needed to produce a fully costed bill, automatically.

Control of timesheets
- Time allotment and analysis
- Reports on missing time / timesheets

Variable dates
Some systems oblige the user to input daily only for that date.

Payroll
General
It is usually much cheaper and more reliable to buy a specialist payroll software package even if the links to the accounting system are not good.

Solicitors do not usually require a sophisticated labour costing from the payroll so manual input of totals is not difficult.

Calculation basis
Time recorded / weekly / monthly.

Payment
Modem links to bank for direct payment / cheque / Post Office / cash / mixed.

Some systems will create Bankers Automated Clearing System compatible tapes.

Integration with nominal ledger
Allows analysis of time / cost over nominal code / cost centre.

Statutory sick / maternity pay calculation

Pension plans

P35 / P45 / P60 / year end and other reports

Staff details
Job / department / holidays due and taken / absence / training / pension / family / previous employment / education.

Company car
Driver(s) / service / accident details with costs.

Confidentiality and security

CONVEYANCING PACKAGES

Conveyancing packages are one of the more prevalent types of support package. Conveyancing is a high-volume area of legal activity characterised by the repetition of a largely sequential series of events, which lends itself to easy automation. Inroads made by licensed conveyancers have been small, but the increased competition has led to a drop in fees in what was the most lucrative market for provincial solicitors.

In order to reduce the unit cost of conveyancing work, and be as competitive as possible, many practices have embraced fully computerised conveyancing systems, allowing higher caseloads per fee-earner and some de-skilling. A critical requirement is to maintain a high quality output. Therefore the settings in automatic and semi-automatic office systems which give rise to exception reports (warning the fee-earner or department manager of problems) and the overall consistency of performance are as important as the ease of use, large storage capacity and ability to carry out many tasks automatically which makes a computer system attractive to the solicitor in the first place.

PACKAGE-SPECIFIC ISSUES

The list of issues below concern the day-to-day operation, use and productivity of conveyancing packages. You should consider the relevance and importance of all of these to your firm when putting together your requirements. Then you can decide which of the packages on offer will best suit your firm.

Case support

Lookup by property address as well as client
Enabling search by previous or prospective property.

Synchronisation of sale and purchase
This option considerably assists in the efficient use of resources and co-ordination of effort.

Automatic update of agents etc. as to case progress
Keeping all parties informed avoids problems and mistakes due to lack of communication.

In-built checks
These can be very useful, e.g. deposit paid before Search. Can you set extra ones yourself if you want?

Images
Maps, drawings and pictures can be scanned and held electronically.

Procedures

Do the standard procedures cover the types of work you do?
For a list of points concerning general matters of procedure design and usability, see the "General Purpose Case Management Packages" section, under "Procedures".

Registered / unregistered

Commercial / domestic

Development site

Estate sales for developer

Lease / freehold

New / existing

Repossession

Sale, purchase

Remortgage

Plot sales

Short term rental

Documents

Can the system produce all the types of documents and forms you need?
Law Society TransAction forms / Search forms / Land Registry forms / other proprietary forms supplied.

*Other word processor compatible precedents /
templates*
E.g. your own style letters / letterheads.

Completion statements
Automatic generation on chosen template, avoiding
duplication of data entry.

Document generation to multiple parties at once
At certain points, when multiple communication is
required, different letters can be automatically
generated.

Facilities

Quotation generation
According to various billing types. Support from
"what if" and historical profit reports compared by
work type, allowing closer costing.

User definable areas of activity / manual override

User definable screens
Especially useful where certain work types are
regularly undertaken, and activities can be devolved to
administrative staff.

Full integration with accounts and client accounts
This allows proper data transfer between time
recording, billing, and client deposit account
reconciliation.

DEBT COLLECTION PACKAGES

This is an area of case support which has seen some automation for a long time. Although there are many different procedures to follow, once embarked on one of them, the procedure can be fairly predictable, albeit with certain "logic forks", where decisions can change the course of the procedure. Significantly, there are several in-house and non-law firm debt collection operations which rely heavily on office and procedure automation systems.

With such competition, the pressures on cost control and quality of service are heavy. Systems must cater directly for your existing clients' business, and any that you have targeted in your future plans, and for this reason demonstrations and tests should be exhaustive. There are many different charging criteria and many different procedures. Developers themselves need to be well acquainted with the business and/or the procedures must be easily amendable to cope with events. Generally the package should have strong central control.

PACKAGE-SPECIFIC ISSUES

The list of issues below concern the day-to-day operation, use and productivity of the package. You should consider the relevance and importance of all of these to your firm when putting together your requirements. Then you can decide which of the packages on offer will best suit your firm.

Basis of claim

Does the system cater for the types of claim you need?
- Goods / services / goods and services
- Professional services
- Work done and materials supplied
- Chattel hire charges
- Unpaid rent
- Insurance premium
- Hire purchase
- Factored account
- Combinations / user-defined

Invoice-based
- Individual / multiple sorted by period / totalled

- Credits cancel earlier invoices / taken by time they occur, interest running

Non-invoice based
Standard / client-defined / manual input wording.

Interest calculation
- Statutory / fixed / variable / different rates on same case
- Simple / compound
- Compounding period definition
- Running balance or amounts outstanding at time of issue

Repossession
- Mortgage: first or second mortgagee
- Residential
- Business
- Public house
- Goods

Dishonoured payments
Cheques / direct debits.

Motor accident (some regard this as a separate topic)
Property / personal injury.

Defended / undefended
Default / on admission / summary judgements.

Detailed standard litigation procedures
- Garnishee
- Warrant of execution / re-issue warrant of execution
- Oral examination
- Attachment of earnings
- Instalment payments
- Warrant of possession / warrant of fieri facias / charging order
- Statutory demand

Insolvency proceedings
Statutory demand / bankruptcy / liquidation.

Solicitors own fees recovery procedure

Reports

General relevance

- Amount outstanding
- Type of work
- Stage of proceedings
- Overdue events
- Size of matter
- Age of matter
- Disbursements
- Recoverable
- Witness and contact details
- Fees and costs

Overall statistical

Matters / debt sizes / collection costs / collection times.

On-screen reports

With sufficient information to deal with telephone enquiries.

Histories

By correspondence / fee-earner / matter / client / period / billing.

Outside agent monitoring

"What if" reports

For bill and interest calculation.

Client reports
- Summarising all matters
- By matter
- By matter where steps taken
- Showing cash fees and disbursements
- Special layouts

Billing

Charge rates

Choice of criteria: scale / individual / percentage

Variable rates required at different stages in the case?

Billing routines

By individual matter / individual client for all matters / time period / costs incurred / funds received.

- Ease of itemisation: c.f. matter history reports
- Automatic or semi-automatic bill production

Bill itemisation
Disbursements / time costs.

Links to accounts package
A very important management consideration. Does the system have an integrated cash book? Are payments recorded automatically in cash book / accounts package?

Will it link with a package from any supplier, or do you have buy this supplier's?

Net or gross billing to clients

Database

Centrally-held data storage
For widely and repeatedly used information.

Client and contact details / court fees and addresses / agents' details including addresses / court officers / private investigators / debtors.

Matter-linked data storage
For information unlikely to be re-used, and therefore not required to be held centrally.

Debtor, witness and claim details / disbursements / recoverable costs / procedural history / billing history / notepad notes / agents / affidavit swearers.

References
User-defined / sufficient space allowed for your own, or your clients' reference style.

Search facilities

Correspondence
- Full view of past documents or details only
- Include log of incoming documents

Payments record
- Money on account
- Instalment payments supported
- Reversal of previous steps where instalment(s) not paid, i.e. re-instigation of court proceedings / issue of threatening letter
- Coping with adjustments to instalments and instalment plans

General Purpose Case Management Packages

This section deals with systems which are tailored by the user or the supplier to cope with a wide variety of types of practice support work. General case management or support systems were developed as an aid to the fee-earner in the conduct and supervision of multiple cases, often handled by a team.

Systems sold as general purpose systems should be distinguished from dedicated systems sold for one particular type of work only (e.g. some conveyancing and debt collection systems). Note that some suppliers have built their specific case support systems using their general purpose engine, demonstrating the possibilities for general application across the legal practice due to the generic nature of some legal activities.

With pressure on costs throughout the profession and incursions from outside the profession on areas of work which have traditionally been solicitors' alone, many practices have seen the automation of their logistical procedures as their salvation. Much can be done with office automation to improve the turnover of the legal practice, but computer technology is no panacea.

Your exact requirements must be assembled over a period of planning and consultation. The advantages and disadvantages of each package on offer must be weighed and potential for surprise must be contained by careful test, referral, demonstration and comparison. When it is finally chosen, the new system must be introduced with care, as the co-operation of the users is essential, especially in areas such as this where the computer can easily be suspected of running the users.

Most of the points discussed here are applicable to dedicated systems as well. To avoid repetition they are discussed here only, so please do read this section as well even if you are only planning on purchasing a dedicated system.

Package-specific Issues

The list of issues below concern the day-to-day operation, use and productivity of the package. You should consider the relevance and importance of all of these to your firm when putting together your requirements. Then you can decide which of the packages on offer will best suit your firm.

Procedures

Standard procedures
Matter type management, with check lists for each case type.

Design of user-defined trains of logic and actions
So that the user can configure the normal work-cycle to suit existing work practices and/or impose a gradated learning curve.

Event and/or date-driven procedures
Automatic / prompt for approval / manual operation, driving the case and supplying exception reports where dates or events are missed or are outside limits.

Where prompt for approval, what are the routines where for some reason approval is not given?

Alteration or overriding of logic and timescales possible
When individual cases do not fit the procedural template, there must be an acceptance by the system of the reality that it is difficult if not impossible to build logic that fits every case.

This must be subject to any security / supervisory interests.

Date overrun
When dates are overrun, how does this affect the timetabling of subsequently listed events? Some events are fixed, such as court dates etc., while others would probably be preferred to be re-scheduled according to the specified timeless.

Configurable procedures
Matter type procedure designs can be changed by the user (according to user security access).

What level of skill is required?

The language involved must be fairly comprehensible, or the normal user will be unable to reconfigure procedures that have evolved.

Procedures robust and flexible

- What is the system response when procedures are not followed entirely?
- Starting halfway through
- Leaving before the end
- Different order of logic
- Leave the procedure and return later
- Something is done and needs reversing later
- Steps left out
- Addresses or other details change
- Importance of memo notes attached to each entity
- Different levels of sophistication can reasonably be expected here according to package price

Event history report

Report on the "events" that have occurred in each case / across the department etc.

Review of matters

Many packages claim to work to Practice Management Standards and/or Legal Aid Franchise Standards. As these are often firm-specific, check what is offered carefully.

Reports

Management requirements

By department, milestone, cost, figures against budget etc.

Statistics

- Number of new matters by type, fee-earner, department over time
- Overruns
- Billings
- Standard costs and timescales for work of each type
- Graphs of trends

Personal requirements

Work in progress, milestones etc.

Search for matter

Is this by code, keyword or free form, i.e. by any part of its title?

Comparisons

Compare factors, e.g. different fee-earners, year's performance.

Logging documents

Document management & tracking by client and matter

"Call up" the client or the matter and see all linked documents.

Document archiving and viewing

Where documents are produced using mail merge automatic document production, these may be visible by looking up the mailing or the recipient details. With imaging technology, this is also now possible with incoming mail, although this is a substantial addition to normal case management systems.

Document storage with a "Review date" for new business

Where Wills etc. are stored and recorded under a document management routine, a review date may be added for marketing, say to remind the client that the document is five years old and may need updating.

Storage under a profiling system may enable a search for types of document, as when affected by a change in the law.

Free text search

For key words through precedent documents.

Fee-earner support

Automatic time entry

Using on screen timing facilities linked to the case management (and often the accounts) package.

Auto-review after no action for a certain time

Trigger on all matters for catching all dormant cases.

Counsel's and expert opinion database

Searchable by free-text and user-defined category.

Case-type specific information

On-line information to ensure the kind of assistance required for high quality work.

Use

Ease of use

So all staff, administrative and fee-earning, can perform more efficiently.

Management overview

Exception reports enable less but more efficient supervision.

Facilities

Interactive client / contact response

Facility to match response / case template to client response / profile, such as highlighting client preferences for telephone contact, or weekly updates, against case profiles that are document intensive or slower moving than the normal business with that client.

MARKETING AND MAILING PACKAGES

Marketing is a new name for something every firm is obliged to do in the course of their business, even as straightforward an action as the sending of Christmas cards to clients and referring contacts. Nowadays many firms see an active approach to the gaining and upkeep of contacts as a logical part of their business strategy, and invitations to open days, newsletters, or advisory notices regarding changes to the law, such as trademarks, are regularly sent out by specific staff with marketing responsibilities. Others have a less organised approach, but nevertheless need to target certain mailshots. The cost, and the negative response which a scatter-gun mailing may raise, militate toward carefully targeted listing for particular purposes. The closer the refinement of your lists and response management, the better marketing as a whole may be justified in terms of your business.

Marketing and mailing are processes applied to a database of contacts. The processes may be applied to a database the firm already has, or a new database. You might buy in a database which has contacts classified in certain ways. The database of contacts and their work history may be built up from work produced with the help of several different systems, often sold separately, in which case data integration will be an issue.

If your system is properly integrated, you can create lists which comprise specific groups of clients defined by your experience of them over a finite length of time. With simpler systems, at least the Christmas cards you sign will be going to clients with whom you specifically have had dealings, with no risk of duplication.

With a sophisticated, integrated system you could choose to offer a seminar on copyright law only to those clients whose business with your particular department concerned publishing and raised over £1,000 in fees in the last three years. You could write your brochure, with a covering letter, and have your own normal letter opening and closing lines (salutations and valedictions) which you use to each client automatically included, or you could have a "responsible partner" for each client whose name could appear on the letter. The system might give you a prior listing so that amendments might be made manually after inspection by a specific list of concerned fee-earners.

Another aspect of this is that the response to each mailing can be monitored, so the next time you use the list, the list members could be refined further by their response to the last mailing. It is clear therefore that lists and mailings form separate entities, the latter dependent on the former. Both have a history: lists have been used in certain mailings (with what response?) and mailings have certain response statistics and amendments against the original list.

Details of responses and attendance at functions may also be used to keep up a client history, comprising more than merely the matters you may have in common, but also their interests and relationships with other contacts and members of staff. This enables a consistent and responsive service to be given to each individual, especially important when holidays interrupt normal lines of contact.

PACKAGE-SPECIFIC ISSUES

The list of issues below concern the day-to-day operation, use and productivity of the package. You should consider the relevance and importance of all of these to your firm when putting together your requirements. Then you can decide which of the packages on offer will best suit your firm.

Database

Names in the database
Where have they come from: other modules or packages, or just those entered in this package?
How are duplicates guarded against?

Details of the names
- Can you hold all you want to?
- How is it entered?
- Is it designed for secretaries and fee-earners, or a marketing department or both?
- Does it expect a contact code?

Lists

How are they made?
Lists are created by the operation of some selection process on names and their attributes as held in the

database. There will be a great deal of information available on some clients from the various packages in an integrated system.

Can the selection ("search") criteria operate on any of the attributes of each name, or only some of them?

Is it easy for your own staff to make up and process new and different criteria according to their own ideas and experience, or are they limited to the ones supplied, or on bespoke (and costly) programming on the supplier's part?

Can there be a large number of different criteria in one selection process, allowing closer accuracy of mailshots?

What can you save about a list?
There are a number of logical possibilities:
- As a list of names and addresses
- As a list of names whose current addresses will be attached when the list is recalled, allowing for intervening update of addresses etc. in other parts of the system
- As a search criterion alone which will self-update the list members when recalled, automatically weeding out lapsed contacts etc.

What can be done with a list?
- Make a mailing
- Make repeated mailings
  Who can use a list? Lists are valuable commercial items: how is their confidentiality preserved?

It is important to keep that personal touch. Who will each letter appear to have come from, and will that person be aware of that?

Does each contact has a corresponding responsible fee-earner? How is that managed by the system? Is your firm able to organise and run such an operation?

What is recorded about lists?
- Usage in mailings
- Success of mailings
  See also mailings, below.

Reports on a list
Automatic / prompted (by period, or on use?) / manual generation of printed lists with addresses

and salutations / valedictions for checking and update.

Expiry date
For deletion of "stale" lists.

Integration

Additional to accounts package, which may only hold clients
Contacts useful for the purpose of marketing or mailing alone may be introduced into the system, such as prospective clients.

Fully integrated with accounts and time recording
In that up-to-date details of matters / fees turnover / responsible partner / addresses and so on can be accessed without manual data input.

Integration of client details throughout firm
Meaning that updates (e.g. client leaves firm) will automatically trickle down to mailing lists used.

Mailing

Mailing response management
- Records of response allow text fields of comments?
- Records for attendance at functions?

Integrated diary system for follow-up

Comprehensive mailshot management

Editing of lists possible

Batched mailings for phased release

Contact data you may want to store

Client?
Yes / No check-box

Date and source of introduction

Financial details

Location
Addresses stored so that they can be sorted by postcode / town / county / country.

Business interests

Business classifications

Responsible partner
Contact salutation and valedictions for all relevant staff.

Contact type
E.g. counsel / client / agent.

Non-clients
Can be entered and held as well: package not limited to people already in list by virtue of their having been entered in another package.
- Matters
- Details on the opposition, case results, etc.

Fees turnover
Integration with accounts saves valuable data search and input time.

Referrals
Full recording of client referral information.

Multiple addresses
For home / holiday / various work bases.

Multiple telephone numbers
For home / holiday / various work bases and mobile phones.

Categories of contact
- Introductory / personal / links
- Specialisations
- Knowledge type

Links
- Displayed as part of both linked contacts' details
- To contacts / staff "known by"
- To organisations "employed by"
- User definable links
- All combinations between individual / organisation

Mailshot history
- Letters sent, responses and results
- Publications sent with follow-up information

- Membership of mailing lists

Leisure interests

Free text narrative
Some packages attach dates to these "text boxes" which are searchable.
    Some allow free text searching on the text itself.

Expert and Counsel register
Nomination of preferred experts in each field with comments.

Archiving
Automatically / prompted according to parameters / manually.

Unlimited numbers of contacts
Test problems of size on search effort. How easy is it to look up a contact on a large database?
    Some firms may want quick look-up to the point where each telephone call may attract an appropriate response without delay.

Deleted / archived matters
Still viewable against client.

Reports
Comparisons
Client type / fee-earner / matter / department, as required.

By branch or consolidated
As well as other report conditions, this may be useful.

Batch reports
Automatic generation of certain groups may be useful, e.g. circulation to all partners of main lists on a regular basis.

Birthday prompts & Christmas card list

Market sectors / priorities

Conflict of interest report
Are you storing all the information you need to make an adequate search?

PRACTICE SUPPORT SYSTEMS

The main functions which may be present can be divided into:

- the accounts system dealing with basic principles of clients, matters, fees, costs (mainly people's time cost), holding client monies, accounting for interest, purchases from suppliers, assets, depreciation, financial reports, management reports, ad hoc reports, statistics, provided to a greater or lesser extent by almost all packages. In some cases this functionality is provided by a non-legal accounting package
- a contact database for marketing and mailing linked to the matter records in the accounting system, around which are built the basic principles of matter record-keeping and statistics, provided by almost all case management and accounting packages. The database is sometimes stand-alone and sometimes part of or linked to a larger firm-wide or accounts database
- a time recording/activity logging module that will keep details of budgets, estimates, work done and steps taken and then produce billing guides and the bill itself and provide information about work in progress. This is sometimes built-in and sometimes linked to another package
- a document production facility using the data from the database to produce template documents and letters as easily as possible, usually through a choice of word processors
- close links with case management software, involvement in the day-to-day actions and steps of the fee-earner: case profile designs with their own logic; links to word processing and forms printing applications; logging retained documents' storage location. These features may help with automatic or semi-automatic logging of time. They are only provided by some case management packages
- the ability for the user, with or without the supplier's help, to build a system to cater for a particular type of work

BENEFITS

The idea is that savings of time and effort are made by:

- only entering data once, with automatic re-use every time it is needed, and a permanent, shared electronic database - avoiding the need for personal address books and diaries, or getting the file to check a piece of information
- sharing information between staff in a department or across the firm
- providing quick on screen look-up of information (e.g. on accounts, names and addresses) for both fee-earners and secretaries
- providing an accessible reminder system for key dates or events in the case process
- keeping an electronic record of the actions taken
- producing useful management information and statistics for the firm and clients
- producing smart, timely, accurate documents as easily and quickly as possible

DATA SHARING

The data sharing aspect leads the system naturally into database organisation of cases, clients and contacts. Obvious questions arise as to whether all such data should be shared between case management, marketing, billing and accounting functions within the firm. One approach is to share all such information. Another is to copy it when required. A third is to keep systems separate. There are pros and cons for each approach, depending on the firm's existing systems and the requirements of each package. Often, total integration is the ideal goal.

REMINDER SYSTEM

An electronic reminder system is usually set up by the user manually (or the system automatically) entering at the time of opening the matter (or during the case) some events, or series of events, usually with their "execute by" dates. There could be events such as "serve notice (by..)" or "court hearing (date)"; they can themselves be entered as a result of events, such as "check for reply (by..)". The reminders appear in the case record, and if dates are attached then some packages display the dates in an electronic diary as well. The attraction of a diary package is that it often provides the most convenient way of keeping abreast of important dates and ensuring they are not missed.

PROCEDURES

Reminder systems can be used in a much more powerful and (for some solicitors) controversial way, actually driving the case, and as such can be effective productivity tools. The idea is that each new matter is assigned a sequence of events sometimes called a procedure. A procedure is a pre-set (either by supplier or user) series of steps or events, usually with timescales included. Then the list of normal events is often loaded in automatically from an appropriate template, flow chart or logic profile.

Although these procedures should always be amendable in the light of each matter's circumstances, when properly set up, they can provide a model series of building blocks from which a similar real case can be built up. Sometimes they also provide a norm against which real cases may be compared, which can be particularly useful for the department or practice manager. Some firms with areas of fairly high-volume, repetitive and time-critical work have found the procedure-based approach facility particularly helpful; where the work is more personal and varied, it may be seen as anathema.

ACTION LOGGING

When letters are written, or other steps are taken, they are usually logged in the matter file, and ticked off the list; the next one is put on it, and so on until the last bill is rendered. This can provide a list of matter-events which may:

- help to satisfy quality assurance and practice management standards by prompting for the correct next step and by recording the actual steps taken
- provide a basis for billing and management accounting and analysis
- be used for a quick "lookup" of the matter to avoid having to actually find the physical file

CHOOSING YOUR SYSTEM

It is not the purpose of this factsheet to define which systems work: the practitioner must follow the usual practice when making any purchase of a critical item: an appropriate balance of defining your needs and matching your needs to what you see, liking the "look and feel" of the system, taking references, buying a tried system, and taking expert advice.

RUNNING DEMONSTRATIONS

Make sure you have a full demonstration. Most demonstrators know the system too well. They will tend to go through the demonstration too fast, without giving you the opportunity to absorb each screen and the information it holds. Make them slow down to your speed: the best option is to get them to demonstrate it with yourself or other prospective users at the keyboard so you determine the speed of each "walk-through".

There will be much that is new and difficult to take in: make sure you get full answers to every point. The system will be with you for a long time, and can either give long-lasting rewards or lingering grief!

Try to get the demonstration done at your premises. This makes possible the trial by all your staff. If they are going to use it, involve them in the decision. If there is any complication, in the use of an electronic telephone book for instance, many users will find it easier to use their own paper one. This involves loss of confidence in the use of the facility and data will be lost to it, since people will not maintain something they don't use. The supplier should already have done all the required testing: if you find any faults, note them down and make sure that a full explanation is given.

Try to get the demonstration done on your equipment. This way the capabilities of the package can be assessed on such things as printer, database, or other compatibility and integration claims the supplier has made.

Finally, weigh the pros and cons carefully: there is a great deal of competition in the market, and you should be able to get exactly what you want.

Test for Usability

Remember that the test is what you think of the package. You are not testing the package for errors, but usability and effectiveness. Does the system offer any real benefits? Will it make the work process easier through streamlining existing practices or providing new tools to do the work? Is there anything about the package you will have to "put up with"? Imagine yourself using the package during a normal day.

- How easy is it to add a new case? Prepare an example for each type of input process
- How easy is it to add a new step or procedure?
- Save the data input. How easy is look-up? Is it all on the same screen?
- How useful is the on screen help?
- How easy is it to correct mistakes or cancel a step?
- Get halfway through a routine input, and then try to reverse out
- Try starting mid-way through a procedure
- Try using "Help" to help
- How much specialist training is needed?
- How reliant on the supplier will you become for changes?
- Have you seen examples of all the types of step you envisage you might require?

The list of issues below concern the strategic issues in the choice of practice support software packages which affect the wider requirements your firm may have when buying a package. The direction is from the general to the specific, and therefore firm-wide "policy" questions arise properly at the start, followed by sections concerning users, general integration, and finally the systems themselves.

Firm-specific Issues
Size of firm

Purpose of the new system
What do you hope to achieve by using the system?

Your budget
- What outlay is reasonable for your firm size and objectives?

- How many firms of your size and/or type use the system?
- Do they use it to the same extent you plan to?

Configuration

Degree of sophistication depending on firm's needs
It is critical that the system does not impose more bureaucracy through its logic requirements than is necessary for your firm's operation, e.g. by enforcing another layer of record keeping, necessary for a large City firm but not a four-partner High Street practice.

Is the screen layout, data content, and throughput suitable for your size and type of practice?

Input options you may require
- Psion organiser option for time recording
- Protem organiser option for time recording
- Central input option (often preferred by larger firms)
- Fee-earner / secretary input option (helps users feel they "own" their data)

Reasonable expansion in use possible in the future
Again, this depends upon the plans of your practice. Remember that a computer system's potential, once realised, can militate for substantial further implementation of IT within an organisation.

Can you buy the basic system now, and "add-ons" later?

Introduction

Suitable for use by administrative staff
Will this package enable less skilled staff to carry out some duties, so fee-earners can perform more efficiently?

Management of change
- How long will changeover take?
- Will "parallel" systems be required for long to cover initial learning?
- How will staff be released for training while also maintaining productivity?
- How will it affect finances?
- Time the introduction, and plan your cash flow carefully, especially where bill production is concerned

Modular / incremental change / phased introduction
Where for some reason installation of an all-embracing package is not required now, make sure you won't need to change the package you are now planning to buy if IT usage within the firm expands in the future.

Security

Password protection
This should prevent unauthorised access, and provide identification of the user to the system. The identification can be used to define the level of access, give details for the "audit trail" kept by the system, or assign personal salutation / valediction values to automatically generated letters.

User-defined security access system
User-defined levels of access, where, say, secretarial staff may have different areas of access-fee from earners, and senior partners from partners, or where practitioners or departments may "own" their own matter data.

If it is important that any user in the firm should not be able to find out whether a client is concerned in a certain matter, great care will have to be taken in checking how security works. Some systems assume that such information should be available to any user, i.e. potentially known throughout the firm. Similar problems may crop up with conflict of interest searches where even the fact the search was made may need to be confidential.

Back-up
This is essential to provide against loss of information. Those responsible for the overall operation of the system should have a tried and tested back-up plan providing for regular back-up of all data or unforeseen events which may result in complete or partial loss of your valuable records.

Audit trail of system transactions
A full audit trail is a mechanism whereby every use of the system is logged along with all changes. It can also trace any exceptions or misuse such as wrong data input etc. A full transaction log is automatically kept by some more expensive databases. A transaction log can enable full reconstruction of data when a data loss (e.g. system crash) has occurred through its addition to previously backed-up files. Otherwise the back-up files will only restore your data to the point in time when the last back-up itself was actually saved, which, with billing information, represents money.

System administration available
This allows the system to be administered by someone, either in terms of regular maintenance, or a more dedicated auditor / maintainer who deals with backing up, audits and archiving, suitable for a large integrated system.

Consider the level of maintenance and administration needed and who will provide it. Will you train someone with a legal background or get a computer specialist?

System administration

Application of parameters across system
Imposing a system-wide regime may be a requirement for security / standards / policy with large systems.
- Who sets up and maintains these settings?
- Does the software need an "administrator"?

Pull-down menus
These should only show the options appropriate to the user's level of access.

Management analysis of transactions
What management overview reports (performance / transactions) are provided? Is there any system-wide imposition of objectives and timescales?

Compliance with practice quality standards
Procedures, logic and record keeping may help your firm comply with quality assurance guidelines such as Legal Aid, Law Society, ISO 9000, BS 5750. Perhaps your practice can comply without extra recording if your system is comprehensive enough. Some systems now claim they specifically address these requirements. Ask referees.

USER-SPECIFIC ISSUES
Interface
Data entry
Ease of use is crucial, but difficult to assess without

speaking to existing users. Speaking to the buyers of the system may not be sufficient. Talk to all types of user.

Input routines should be carefully examined for duplication in data entry. There should be no increase over present routines: the best result is that less qualified staff may do it in less time than at present.

Bar code input possible

Easier, quicker and more accurate input of data, usually from pre-printed labels, e.g. file details, client codes.

Error recovery

How easy is it to recover from errors?

Are you locked into a data entry routine with no way to back out until its cycle is concluded, leaving a wrong or empty entry in the database?

Drill down to transaction detail

The facility to "zoom in" from, say, matter details to the list of documents, and then perhaps to the details of one of the documents, and then to the details of the sender of that document, following the trail as can be done with paper books.

"Friendliness"

A broad impression provided by many things including the two points above. Largely imparted by the clear presentation of relevant data (with no irrelevant data) on an uncluttered screen. Usually better with a Graphical User Interface, but ease of navigation around the system, support for change of course and change of inputs (error correction) also play a role.

Graphical User Interface (GUI)

Windows, DOS, character or graphics?

Some systems will produce mixed interfaces depending on the terminal configuration. Is the package offered to run on existing hardware; are you happy with the look of the interface?

Mouse support

Or "point and click". Although less critical when users are more familiar with the package, this capability significantly increases ease of use.

If you want look-up facilities which only require mouse operation (for technophobes who are reluctant to go as far as input) this is probably essential. This is not available on dumb terminals.

Facilities

Macros for repetitive operations

Macros are used to cause a series of pre-recorded commands to be repeated automatically. It is often useful to be able to build your own macros.

Notepad

This is a facility for entry of comments or case summary at different points through the case, like attaching a "sticky" to a file page. Some packages even allow a search on these comments, to pick up key words and help you find your place.

Context sensitive help

This becomes less of an issue as time goes on following introduction, but in the early stages the difficulties of the new user are more easily resolved if they have the increased likelihood of "help yourself" advice afforded by this facility. If it is offered, try it yourself to test its usefulness.

Support

Training

Training will be necessary where changes are to be made to work practices yet a smooth transition is required. This should be expressly provided by the supplier. Will this be on site, on your own data? Ask to speak to other users who have been trained.

If the system requires a high level of expertise, the number of personnel who need training must be enough to cover for illness and holidays. Moreover, the staff who are not regularly using the system must be kept up to date so they can cope with contingencies.

Support for usage problems

After installation and training what support does your supplier envisage and will it be adequate for your requirements (a question for your referees)?

Upgrades provided under software maintenance contract

- What provision for upgrading is made by your supplier?

● What are their plans for change and development?

● Do they guarantee support for this particular product over its projected lifetime?

Dial-up links for support

Dial-up access for support is very common. Are all calls logged? Are you in control of access? Who pays for calls? What security is offered against unwanted intruders?

Manuals

Most systems require manuals for learning the package in depth. Manuals help ease learning for new recruits. Look at manuals and test them for readability. Check they are all up to date.

INTEGRATION ISSUES
System

Windows compatibility

Does the package run on Windows 3.x? This is relevant where other considerations demand it, such as existing or planned use of software (such as word processing) which is reliant on this interface.

For new or soon to upgrade users, there is the extra consideration of Windows '95 compatibility.

Network or single user; integrated or stand-alone

This is normally a relatively straightforward decision, but do bear in mind the issue of future expansion: only some packages will support many configurations.

Existing hardware/OS/network type compatibility

Will new equipment be required or will the package operate successfully on your hardware / operating system / network; is the package compatible with your printers and fonts?

Are your referees running the same kind of equipment?

What was their experience of the supplier's management of this issue?

Portability across platforms

A computer operating system / hardware / network combination is often termed a platform. Will the package run on a different platform if you require this in the future? Some packages offer very much more flexibility in this area than others.

Data independence

This means that the data which you input is kept in a structure which is not exclusively dedicated to the particular package you are using, so that if you change the package you use, or the developers go out of business, the data can be lifted from the database for use by another package.

You will be unable to move the data if it is locked into formats which are unknown to others when that process takes place. The dislocation in your business could be considerable.

Industry standards in data formats are relevant in determining just how portable the data can be.

Does the package utilise a well-known database (such as Oracle, Access, Microsoft SQL Server) for underlying data management?

Data independence is often promised but be warned that this is the biggest area for problems. Many supplier / user disputes arise over access to data. Many users have found it very difficult to extract their data in a usable way when they want.

If you let someone lock up your data, make sure you know you have a key and you know it works in case they become unable or unwilling to help you.

Export / import of data in standard format

In theory this enables different suppliers' packages to be used in combination on the same system, but is rarely as simple as it sounds.

It entails rearranging the data from one package to a standard format, and then moving it into another package, possibly rearranging it again for the user package. This can involve costs in time and inaccuracy.

Data

Update across the system

If this is given as a feature, data entry in one area will automatically update all related / dependent items within the package. For example entry of a client meeting to discuss a new matter will automatically / by prompt open a new matter, post the timing details, log the meeting (and possibly its record), ask for the next step(s) and enter them in your scheduler, or for accounts, payment in will update the bank account, income ledger column and client and matter balances according to its posting.

Access to other work-related packages

Transfer of data between the packages used should be possible, although in some cases incompatible data structures will not allow this. Often the cost of development required to interface accurately with someone else's software will effectively prohibit its use.

Automatic update between packages in a system

Once only data entry / update of data from one package to another. For example if a client pays their bill, the update in the accounts management area will also update the details of that person as accessed by case management. This should be automatic if all data is held once only (in one place) and is accessed by each part of the system when it is needed.

Avoids duplication of input, and allows data re-use. Sometimes updates are by data exchange rather than shared data. Data exchange between packages may be manual or automatic. Automatic may be of direct, data-compatible, or "flat file" type. Some formats make true integration slow and search over certain application-mixed criteria problematic.

Client details used for new matter because of data sharing

Where existing clients' details are automatically displayed as the default for their new cases without the need to input them again.

Validation of critical data entry

If accuracy is critical, checking of input data according to pre-determined "validation" rules may be required, and system designs should offer this.

Diary

Scheduler / memo notes

Date type data with associated text from other applications automatically copied over to the diary scheduler. Some packages attach memo notes for easier identification.

Reminders / action charts / "to do" lists

Dates from case management details can be automatically / by prompt / manually put on the staff member's "to do" list. For partners, fee-earners, and assistants: diaries for forthcoming events / progress reports. Some packages offer diary-driven / event-driven option for list makeup.

Overview of schedules and action charts

By supervisor, supported by search routines. A wide variety of search and enquiry facilities are supplied with the different packages.

Adjustments / redirection of workload for holidays / illness

Automatic (on pre-set criteria) reallocation of work when a member of staff is absent.

Repetition of diary entries possible

E.g. regular matter reviews can be entered in the diary for many dates at once.

Option for cashflow forecast events

So that costly activities can be appropriately timetabled.

Industry standards

Will the diary and/or scheduler interface to highly functional and very powerful emerging industry standards used by the computing majors such as Microsoft, Novell/WordPerfect, IBM/Lotus, Digital and others?

Packages

Existing software

See item on data export and import (above) concerning existing data.

Questions here concern needless data input duplication; possibilities for data disagreement (the right hand not knowing what the left hand is doing); compatibility with your preferred word processor and existing precedents.

Integrated with accounts and time recording

The most frequent form of greater integration into firm-wide systems, although the nature of those links should be properly understood by the buyer.

Fully integrated might mean where linked client, contacts, accounts, billing and case management systems exist with a shared pool of data. This offers the possibility of powerful firm-wide searches and reports on the information, a single firm-wide contact management and marketing system, due to the existence of the data, offering the reward of an improved marketing effort co-ordinated across the firm.

Contrast the advantages of this with a series of separate databases each with details of their contracts, cases, time and so on.

Links to payroll

Staff details automatically re-used in salary calculation. Expenses automatically added to payroll amounts and posted in ledgers.

Apportionment of fees may be one of your requirements.

Download to spreadsheets wp or database packages possible

Data is / can be configured for transfer to (usually PC-based) spreadsheet or database for wider viewing and broader manipulation, including DIY graph production, or inclusion in word processing or desk top publishing production.

Communications ready

For easy connection to internal and/or external communications systems.

Communication

Dial-up links with third party

Links may be used for:

- E-mail links to clients, counsel and others
- Electronic links with software suppliers for on-line update support and diagnosis
- Electronic access to data feeds from data provision of stock market and currency information
- Electronic access to on-line search databases (e.g. credit agencies, legal case and know-how databases)
- Modem access allows complete file and data transfer. Some packages use a private protocol to cover security interests in this situation

ISDN dial-up

Provides a very fast dial-up capability often virtually equivalent to the speed of a leased line. The economics depend on the average daily connect time, the volume of the data being transferred and the distances involved.

Direct fax

Straight from the computer connection to the phone line, with no waiting for the paper feed.

Note that single-user and network systems are available.

Direct faxing to the desk is also available from some suppliers. It may use a DDI extension to route the fax round your internal network.

E-mail

Especially for intra-company communication. Such links may be temporary dial-up or permanent, leased line.

Psion organiser link

For practices where the users need to input away from the terminal, a hand-held electronic organiser can be used to input time details, text etc. which is then connected to the terminal for downloading.

SYSTEM-SPECIFIC ISSUES

These matters concern the general functional sophistication of the package. Clearly more sophistication tends to increase costs, although this need not always be the case.

Database - nature

Access to confidential information

Following on from password and access issues, this point concerns whether the package you want to buy has the capability to manage confidentiality in the way that suits you.

Relational database

A "buzzword", but an important one. The relationships in your database describe many of the constraints which define your data. Without these relationships being expressly and adequately described, major inaccuracies can occur. Therefore, although a database being relational is better in principle, much depends on the design, so being "relational" does not mean it is perfect.

Archiving

This is an important issue which determines the behaviour of some of your database. In the future the sheer number of matters in the database may create their own overhead. With searches the search time may lengthen or they may simply return information that is out of date. A move of elderly data from the "current matters" lists may be beneficial. This should be addressed by the system design.

Real-time updating / batch processing

Does data input update the main database immediately and/or in an "after hours" batch operation?

Real-time updating is important for the system that has many users who need accurate information from the database.

Batch input may be helpful where large scale data input is carried out externally, e.g. under contract.

Random posting of varying transaction types

Allows entry to the system and input of data in any sequence i.e. "out of time" / out of pattern.

User-configurable settings in data entry

The ease and extent of configurability varies enormously. One example on offer is user-definable fields for data entry: case profiles / categorisation; milestones; client profiles etc.

System limits

Some systems control licensing by limiting the number of active matters, contracts etc.

Having no limits avoids the need to archive but may increase search times as the system ages.

Unlimited numbers of data items

Where this is listed as a feature, it may allow unlimited addresses, numbers, salutation / valedictions etc.

Sometimes systems have inadequate, arbitrary limits.

Undertakings

Some systems provide a formal way of logging and monitoring the giving and receiving of undertakings. If this is important to your firm examine the detail of what is offered, what is recorded and how the reminders work.

Data access

Drill-down access to detailed data

Enables the user to use data "stepping stones" to zoom in from, say, matter details to the list of documents and correspondence created for the matter, and then perhaps to the details of one of the documents, and then to the details of the sender of that document, as would be done with physical files, or for accounts, income column total to individual payments to client / matter history.

Most important for unstructured search and error / exception tracking.

Search and enquiry relevance and accessibility

This is the direct user interface for recalled information, carried out by a "search" of the database, according to your "enquiry".
- How are ad hoc enquiries catered for?
- Are the supplied enquiries adequate / useful?
- Where the user has made a particular search, can a report of the result be run?

Subdivision of fields in search
- How specific can a search be?
- E.g. by user or matter specific data

Quick look-up of user-relevant details

How easy is it to make a quick look-up, say to quickly refresh your memory when a client calls (e.g. identification of client history and profile)?

Save search criteria for re-use

Some systems allow search results (the actual data you dug up) to be saved.

Some allow the search criteria (the way you dug it up) to be saved for later re-use. The choice becomes more important when updates are required.

Query generation

Is it possible to add your own searches; what level of skill is needed?

After the initial installation and training period, the complexity of compilation of new enquiries ought not to put them outside the abilities of the well-motivated user.

Example enquiries

These are usually supplied to cover the "most usually asked questions" of the database, giving a basic collection of system reports, and also provide an example for self-generated reports.

Reports

Routine and exception reports are needed: ask for and look at the supplier's report pack.

Various reports may be automatically/prompted/ manually generated as required.

Certain types should be standard, such as year end figures.

Build your own reports

Is it possible to write your own reports; what level of skill is needed?

Writing your own reports means "programming" the computer to perform an operation. Languages which are specially made for ease of understanding tend to trade ease of use for real functionality.

Are links provided to printing / word processing, or can DIY report results only be seen on screen?

Who in your firm will need to build / tailor their own ad hoc and regular reports?

When is specialist help needed for a report be "tailor-made" for the customer?

Report preview on screen

It is often convenient to be able to preview a report on screen before deciding whether to print it. Some systems offer this.

Can all reports be printed?

Visual / audible warnings

Graphical representation

Allows preparation of charts and graphs from data, e.g. showing comparisons between this year and last in terms of income.

Transfer to WP package possible

For standard (template) / manual letter production and data manipulation.

Word processing

Integrated document generation

Properly implemented this enables seamless links to your favourite word processor with details of matter / receiver / sender transferred to the document itself, for both templates and non-standard letters.

Some document production is event- and/or date-driven.

Systems that generate documents through their own editor can often not take advantage of your usual set of word-processor fonts.

Levels of word processor interaction

Manual: transfer to WP application with non-automatic document production.

Includes production of all standard forms - normal use of templates for repeated production of the same letters and documents. Without this typewriters may still prevail.

Mail merge facility to WP application, with automatic data transfer (e.g. name, address and other case specific details) to document templates.

Mail merge with prompt (by date or event) from case management logic routines and document review. What are the routines where for some reason approval is not given?

Completely system-generated document production without review (suitable for more predictable / repetitive document and matter types).

Printout of file copy / report at same time as document

Sometimes this may be required for file or work practice purposes.

Templates

Pre-configured sets of documents, forms and procedures

These should ideally be supplied with the package, although costs should be monitored here.

Does the package offer all the documents and procedures you will need? Who originated these -

another user, the supplier or someone else? Is their understanding of the law and practice accurate and detailed enough for your work?

Re-configuring some systems is very time consuming.

Templates amendable
- Easily?
- At user / group / client / system level, so different users can have their own dedicated templates?
- Single documents amendable: possible to include personalised additions?

Adjusting existing relevant precedents or templates
Where your firm already has its own templates, these should be made compatible. What needs to be done and by whom?

Sample documents
It is useful to have these for prospectus / client demonstration purposes.

Printing

Printer support
Some packages do not work easily with some printers and fonts: check this in advance and check whether your supplier will deal with this on installation.

Changes to layout which may become necessary (e.g. for new stationery) can be difficult and time-consuming.

Check the rated throughput of printers that could be in continuous use against present / projected / possible use.

Duplex
For documents where double-sided printing is needed, e.g. affidavits.

Use of plain paper
Use plain paper instead of specially-produced letterheads and electronic forms for Court documents to save on costs.

Use of pre-printed forms
Your firm may use pre-printed forms: will the

printing system be configurable to work with these / easily re-configurable when their layout changes?

It is best to try to replace these with electronic versions.

Colour printing
- Is this required?
- Are the resolution and colours offered to a high enough standard?

Multi-paper types and bins
Support for printers with several paper trays for different document types.

If this can be done from the same printer, although printers themselves may be more expensive if they need extra paper bins, fewer will be needed in total.

Queued or instant
- Can be sorted in queue: by contact / destination / paper type
- May be more efficient to use printing facilities after hours
- Usually only large scale operations will benefit from queued "batch" printing

Cheque printing

Labels
- For files / addresses
- Do these labels work with your printer?

Printout at any time
No need to exit the work module you are in at the time.

WILLS, TRUST AND PROBATE PACKAGES

Wills, trust and probate systems encompass several different systems, often sold separately. While trust accounting of matters is supported more from accounting type packages, they should be designed for use by fee-earners and not the firm's cashiers. Will production is more of a document assembly/word processing application as it mainly concerns drafting and document logging. Case management issues are included where diary reminders for action and letter generation are concerned. Probate work is more like other case management work, although again requiring accounts support. Probate systems are developed as an aid to the fee-earner in the conduct and supervision of multiple cases, often handled by a team. Keeping up to date with tax advice and other changing areas of the law may be an additional requirement.

The main requirements for a probate package are similar to those for other support packages. There needs to be a database of contacts (clients, beneficiaries and other parties), the ability to automatically generate letters at various stages of a matter and the ability to keep track of the various papers and documents in a matter.

Specific features for a wills and probate package include: the ability to manage and track wills and deeds for all clients, the ability to keep records relating to the assets of an estate including financial assets, chattels and other property and the ability to transfer information from pre-existing computer records such as a wills register or database into the probate. A useful extra would be some form of tax calculation or advisory module for tax planning purposes and for capital gains tax purposes.

Some probate systems include facilities for automatically recording the information necessary to produce estate accounts including assets, income, liabilities, expenses and bequests and some also produce the actual accounts.

The correspondence and document production module is important, not least from a point of view of what standard documents are included. For instance the system may include over one hundred letters plus the facility to generate oaths. You should look carefully at the text of the documents that will be produced by

any system you shortlist and compare that with the text that you tend to use in your own firm. As mentioned in the general section on support packages, you should check whether you can add documents of your own and change the sample documents.

The style of operation of the software is also important. Comprehensive security against unauthorised access to data is especially important for a probate package.

To summarise, a comprehensive system should embrace will drafting, a will register, a database of contacts (executors, beneficiaries, asset holders, creditors, registries, valuers, brokers etc.), the production of grants of probate and letters of administration with will annexed, special grants, production of oaths including testator details together with use of a standard word processor, comprehensive database facilities, client accounting, trust accounting and tax advice.

It will also help the busy practitioner if the system can produce its own billing guides and integrates with the accounts and time recording packages from the same supplier.

PACKAGE-SPECIFIC ISSUES

The list of issues below concern the day-to-day operation, use and productivity of the package. You should consider the relevance and importance of all of these to your firm when putting together your requirements. Then you can decide which of the packages on offer will best suit your firm.

Configuration
See the Accounting section for details of configuration etc.

Logging documents
Document management and tracking by client and matter
"Call up" the client or the matter and see all linked documents.

Storage and viewing

Where documents are produced using mail merge automatic document production, these may be visible by looking up the mailing or the recipient details.

With imaging technology, this is also now possible with incoming mail, although this is a substantial addition to normal case management systems.

Storage of documents with a "Review date" for new business

Where wills etc. are stored and recorded under a document management routine, a review date may be added for marketing, say to remind the client that the document is five years old and may need updating.

Storage under a profiling system may enable a search for types of document, as when affected by a change in the law.

Free text search

For key words in the main text of precedent documents.

Deeds database

Record card with basic details of each deed

- Details / full description
- Deed type
- Special clauses
- Value
- Creation and amendment dates
- Reminder / brought forward dates
- Drafting fee-earner
- Archive position / holder's address
- Movements log
- Land registry number(s)
- Link to client / matter reference
- Link to other deeds
- Property addresses
- Date of receipt
- Depositor and holder's details and address

Will drafting

Will drafting facility

- Supporting the two-stage process
- Collecting the facts from the client
- Will processing

Set up testator, executors, beneficiaries, third parties etc.

Standard wills or will clauses

User builds own selection or system asks questions and builds the will.

Diagrams to illustrate wills

Produce bill with the will

Can a straightforward will be produced on a single client visit?

Will database

Record cards

- With basic details of each will for quick look-up by parties: testator, executor, beneficiaries, dependants and other third parties
- Details / full description
- Type
- Special clauses
- Value
- Amendment dates, codicils
- Reminder / brought forward dates
- Drafting fee-earner
- Archive position / holder's address
- Movements log
- Link to client / matter reference
- Link to other wills
- Discretionary trust flag

Log by actual precedent / categorised clauses

Retrieve the will by its content, so legal changes affecting particular measures can be semi-automatically processed.

Probate

Set up

Parties: testator, executor, beneficiaries, dependants and other third parties.

Identification of assets and liabilities

- Cash in hand
- Accounts
- Stocks and other interests
- Assurances

- Pensions and salaries
- Chattels
- Rents due
- Foreign and real property
- Solely / nominated / jointly owned
- Debts / claims
- Income
- Inheritance and CG tax
- Funeral costs

Calculation of tax liability prior to death

Adjustments to values

Payments in and out
Fees / IHT instalments / relief against sale losses.

Preparation of the Inland Revenue account

Probate registry

Insolvent estates
Personal representative liabilities / expiry of notice for claims.

Sale of property during administration
- Land registry fees
- Landlords agents' fees
- Estate agents' commission
- Legal costs
- Net proceeds

Clearance certificate

Modifying provisions under will or intestacy

Estate distribution

Client account

Compliance with practice quality standards
Do procedures, logic and record keeping comply with quality assurance guidelines, e.g. Law Society, ISO 9000, BS 5750?

Prevention of overdrawing
What messages or overrides are used?

Notional or designated deposit account interest calculation
Calculation of interest on divisions of larger deposits / as a sum of a portfolio of investments. Actual interest / interest due according to guidelines.

Are there sufficient bands and rates for your purposes?

Can the calculations be made at any time on a single matter or a group of matters?

Probate and trust accounts

Trust accounts
What options are offered?

Schedule of assets / capital

Modifications
- Scrip issues / rights issues
- Acquisitions and disposals

Income / dividends

Expenses

Valuations
CGT and IHT

Draft accounts

Final accounts

Investments

Valuation on holdings
By client / client group / custodian.

Dividend reports / contract notes

Broker reports

Facilities

Links to third party financial databases

Tax advice

Cost / benefit "what if" reports

CGT / inheritance tax / VAT / grant
Advice and calculation.

Updated regularly
Support required.

Reports

Assets / income / liabilities / expenses / bequests

On-line viewing of copy

Comparisons
Client or client group / fee-earner / year / department, as required.

By branch or consolidated
As well as other report conditions, this may be useful.

Batch reports
Automatic generation of certain groups may be useful.

SUPPLIER INDEXES

IS IT A BIRD? IS IT A PLANE?
NO. IT'S
KESTREL SOLICITORS ACCOUNTS

Now available through Windows & Windows 95

Also available in DOS

Does your practice want a highly advanced and reliable accounts system?
Are you fed up with paying too much for legal software?
Are you a practice with between 1 and 25 fee earners?

If you answered yes to any of the above then why not see the system through your own Windows - for FRE

- -

If you would like some more information or a demonstration disk please contact Alison Bagnall
on 01565 755154 or return this form by fax on 01565 633807.

Name _____ Position _____

Address _____

_____ Post Code _____

DX _____ Telephone _____ Fax _____

Laserform M.D. Barry Hawley-Green receives his award from Lord W

More Quality Software from Laserform Law

LAB 7

DOCUMENT ASSEMBLY SYSTEMS

ELECTRONIC PUBLISHING

FINANCIAL SERVICES

INFORMATION MANAGEMENT

BIBLIOGRAPHY

1 LAW OF COMPUTERS AND INFORMATION TECHNOLOGY

1.1 General works

1.1.1 UPDATED WORKS

Charlton SNL (ed) (1988-)
Encyclopaedia of Data Protection *Sweet and Maxwell*
ISBN 0421369000

Rennie, M (1994-)
Computer contracts *Sweet and Maxwell*
ISBN 0421490500

Saxby, Stephen (ed) (1990-)
Encyclopaedia of information technology Law *Sweet and Maxwell*
ISBN 0421372109

Smedinghoff, Thomas J (1994-)
Multimedia legal handbook: a guide from the Software Publisher's Association *Wiley*
ISBN 0471109932

Tapper, CF and Lehmann, M (1993-)
A handbook of European software law *Oxford University Press*
ISBN 0198257546

Walkley, G (1994-)
Negotiating technical assistance agreements and technology licences *International Business Library*
ISBN 0898769087 (Comes with disk)

1.1.2 TEXTBOOKS

Anderson, Mark S (1995)
Technology: law of exploitation and transfer *Butterworth*
ISBN 0406013047

Bainbridge, David I (1995)
Introduction to computer law 3rd ed *Pitman*
ISBN 0273619403

Bainbridge, David I (1994)
Software copyright law 2nd ed *Butterworth*
ISBN 040604841X

Bainbridge, David I (1995)
Software licensing *Central Law Training Professional Publishing*
ISBN 1858110289

Black, Trevor (1995)
International licensing and protection of computer software *NCC & Blackwell*
ISBN 1855544148

Boss, AM and Rutter, JB (1993)
Electronic data interchange agreements: a guide and source book *Kluwer Law and Taxation*
ISBN 9284211522

Burgunder, L (1994)
Legal aspects of managing technology *South-Western Publishers*
ISBN 0538826649 (US)

Burnett, Ken (1995)
Software licensing: a guide to selected sources *Chartered Institute of Purchasing and Supply*
ISBN 0900607920

Byrne, NJ (1994)
Licensing technology *Macmillan Press*
ISBN 0333531493

Carr, Indira and Williams, KS (1995)
Computers and law *Ablex*
ISBN 1567501710 (US)
(Also published by Intellect ISBN 1871516358)

Cavazos, E and Morin, G (1995)
Cyberspace and the law *MIT Press*
ISBN 0262531232 (US)

Downing, R (1995)
EC information technology law *Chancery Law Publishing*
ISBN 0471950491

Drexl, J (1994)
What is protected in a computer program?
Copyright protection in the United States and
Europe *VCH*
ISBN 3527286888

Evans, N (1995)
Understanding European product compliance
legislation: definitive guide to understanding
European compliance issues for information
technology and telecommunication products
Genesys Telecom
ISBN 1898811024

Franklin, C (1995?)
Business guide to privacy and data protection
2nd ed *Kluwer Law and Tax*
ISBN 9065447245 (* May not be published yet)

Galbraith, A (1994)
Law for business technology and computing
Butterworth-Heinemann
ISBN 0750621516

Galler, BA (1995)
Software and intellectual property protection:
copyright and patent issues for computer and
legal professionals *Quorum*
ISBN 0899309747 (US)

Harris, Thorne D (1994)
Software developer's complete legal companion
Prima Publishing
ISBN 1559585021 (US)

Henry, Michael (1994)
Publishing and multimedia law *Butterworths*
ISBN 040603768X
(Contains precedents + 3.5 disk)

**International Audit and Consultancy Services
(1994)**
Information technology: new nitty gritty guide
Cronus
ISBN 0952450852

Janasoff, S (1995)
Science at the bar: law, science and technology in
America *Harvard University Press*
ISBN 0674793021 (US)

Jones, P and Marsh, D (1994)
Essentials of EDI law *Blackwell*
ISBN 1855544296

Katch, ME (1995)
Law in a digital world *Oxford University Press*
ISBN 0195080173

Klinger, Paul and Burnett, Rachel (1994)
Drafting and negotiating computer contracts
Butterworth
ISBN 0406156050

Lloyd, Ian A and Simpson, Moira (1995)
Law on the electronic frontier *Edinburgh
University Press*
ISBN 0748605940

Mackaay, E et al (ed) (1995)
Electronic superhighway: the shape of technology
and law to come *Kluwer Law International*
ISBN 9041101357

Marchese, DL (1994)
Business licensing agreements *Longmans*
ISBN 0851216587

Michael, James (1994)
Privacy and human rights: an international and
comparative study, with special reference to
developments in information technology
Dartmouth Publishing Co.
ISBN 1855213818
(Also published by UNESCO ISBN 9231028081)

Morgan, R (1995)
Computer contracts *FT Law and Tax*
ISBN 0752001612

National Computer Centre Legal Group (1994-)
Legal guidance notes for IT management *National
Computer Centre*

Reed, C (1995)
Computer law 3rd ed *Blackwells*
ISBN 1854314483

Reed, C and Davies, L (1995)
Digital cash: the legal implications *IT Law Unit,
Centre for Commercial Studies, Queen Mary &
Westfield College University of London (Research
project)*

Rubin, H (ed) (1995)
International technology transfers *Graham and Trotman*
ISBN 1859661750

Russell, KV and Jones, R (1994)
International yearbook of law computers and technology *Carfax Publishing Co.*
ISBN 0902879502

2 Computing Books Directly Relevant to Law

2.1 Computer suppliers/information technology guides

Law Society Practice Advice Service (1994)
Computer suppliers list *Law Society*

Lindon Wood Management Consultants Ltd (1995-)
Guide to information technology for lawyers *Lindon Wood Management Consultants Limited* (Regina House, 1 Victoria Street, Liverpool, L2 5QA) (Updated Quarterly)

2.2 Document imaging

Queen Mary & Westfield College London University, Centre for Commercial Law Studies (1994)
Guide to the legal implications of document image processing systems *Society for Computers and Law*

2.3 Litigation support

Eyres, PS (1996)
Smart litigating with computers: the complete step by step guide to computer applications for the nineties and beyond (Paralegal law library series) *Wiley*
ISBN 0471592285

Mital,V (ed) (1995)
Advanced litigation support and document imaging *Kluwer Law International*
ISBN 9041101136 (UK and US)

Smith, Graham JH (1994)
Lawyer's guide to litigation support 2nd ed *Society for Computers and Law*
ISBN 090612228

Strizek, NF, Siemer, DL and Land, NS (1994)
Manual of litigation support databases: 1994 cumulative supplement *Wiley*
ISBN 0471307602 (US)

2.4 Legal datbases and CD-ROMs: directories and online search aids

This is a rapidly changing area and books are out of date before they are published. The relevant on-line hosts will publish their own directories, and articles about relevant sources of information are also published in sources such as the journal *Computers and Law.*

CD-ROM directory: the complete guide to CD-ROM and multimedia titles (1996) *TFPL*
ISBN 0333662555

Heels, Erik J (1996)
Internet legal resources on the world wide web: the top 500 essential web sites for legal issues and information *Ventura*
ISBN 1566043166 (US)

Nichols, Sarah J (1993)
CD-ROM and online law databases 4th ed *ASLIB*
ISBN 0851422985

McKnight, Jean Sinclair (1995)
LEXIS companion: a complete guide to effective searching *Addison-Wesley*
ISBN 0201483351

Rosenfeld, Louis, Janes, J and Vander Kolk, M (ed) (1995)
Internet compendium: subject guides to social sciences, business and law resources *Mansell*
ISBN 0720123054

Venables, Delia and Christian, Charles (1995-)
Guide to Internet for lawyers. Venables, 10 Southway, Lewes, Sussex, BN7 1LU

3 BOOKS ON COMPUTERS AND APPLICATIONS SOFTWARE

There are thousands of books on basic computing, mostly current (i.e. current to the latest update of the computer package concerned). Many of these are guides for the general user, which would be of relevance to anyone wishing to learn about the topic/software in question. It is quite impossible within the timescale to list them all. It is also a matter of very personal choice which book is best for any one reader.

In general:

1 Check carefully that the book covers the latest version of the software and also the relevant operating system (Windows 3.1, 3.11, Windows '95, Apple Mac etc.)

2 Browse through a selection of different guides to see which is the most suitable for you. Any large book shop should have a good selection.

The following series cater for beginners:

Microsoft Publishing "step by step" guides
They really do provide a step by step guide. Very clearly set out. They also have a training disk, which contains examples which can be used by the user when working through the exercises.
An example is:
Catapult (1994)
Microsoft Office for Windows step by step
ISBN 1556156480

IDG Books Worldwide "for Dummies" series
Chatty, informal style, with some American slang. Some of the later editions come with floppy disks containing exercises.
An example is:
Gookin, Dan (1996)
Word 6 for Windows for dummies *IDG Books Worldwide*
ISBN 1568846282 (Comes with 3.5" floppy disk)

Que (or sometimes Alpha Books) "Complete Idiot's guide" series
Very American, with a chatty informal style. Contains some American slang.

An example is:
Gold, L (1995)
Complete idiot's guide to Excel for Windows 95 International version
ISBN 0789706407

Ziff-Davis Press "PC Learning Labs" series
Similar to Microsoft Press books in that they provide a clear step by step guide. They also contain a teaching floppy disk containing exercises).
An example is:
Reber, S (1995)
PC learning labs teaches Word Pro 96 for Windows 3.1 *Ziff-Davis Press*
ISBN 1562762249
The series does not seem to cover as many software packages as Que or IDG.

4 SPECIFIC SUBJECTS OR APPLICATIONS SOFTWARE

4.1 EDI

Blacker, K (1994)
Basics of electronic data interchange in smaller companies *Edistone Books*
ISBN 1897815026

Blacker, K and O'Coy, A (1994)
Basics of electronic data interchange *Edistone Books*
ISBN 1897815042

Boss, AM and Rutter, JB (1993)
Electronic data interchange agreements: a guide and source book *Kluwer Law and Taxation*
ISBN 9284211522

European Construction Institute (1994)
Data transfer and EDI 2 vols *European Construction Institute*
ISBN 1873844263
(Vol 1 is an introduction to EDI)

Harris, B (ed) (1994)
EDI yearbook 1995 *Blackwell*
ISBN 1855545500

Krcmar, H et al (ed) (1995)
EDI in Europe: how it works in practice *Wiley*
ISBN 0471953547

Paraiso, D (1995)
Implementing EDI *HW Sams*
ISBN 0672308312 (US)

Solok, PK (1994)
From EDI to electronic commerce: a business
initiative 2nd ed *McGraw-Hill*
ISBN 0070595127 (US)

Yiannopoulos, AN (1995)
Ocean bills of lading: traditional forms,
substitutes and EDI systems *Nijhoff*
ISBN 0792333616

4.2 Marketing

Gorski, D and Ingram, J (1994)
Sales and marketing software handbook *Pitman*
ISBN 0273606158

Settle, C (1995)
Cyber marketing *Ziff-Davies Press*
ISBN 1562763288 (US)

4.3 CD-ROMS

Bradley, Phil (1994)
Going online and CD-ROM 9th ed *Aslib*
ISBN 08514232X

Bradley, Phil and Webb, Sylvia (1994)
CDROMs: how to set up your work station *Aslib*
ISBN 0851423310

Rathbone, A (1995)
Multimedia and CD-ROMS for dummies 2nd ed
IDG Books Worldwide
ISBN 1568849087

4.4 Networks

Bobola, Dan (1995)
Complete idiot's guide to networking *Alpha Books*
ISBN 15676615902

Lowe, Doug (1994)
Networking for dummies *IDG Books Worldwide*
ISBN 1568840799

Robinson, L (1995)
Installing a local area network *Aslib*
ISBN 0851423388

4.5 Electronic Mail

Collins, S (1995)
Electronic mail: a practical approach *Butterworth-Heinemann*
ISBN 0750621126

Pride, Simon (1994)
E-mail for librarians *Aslib*
ISBN 0851423329

4.6 Internet

Butler, Mark (1995)
How to use the Internet 2nd ed *Ziff-Davis Press*
ISBN 1562763482

Crumlish, C (1996)
Internet for busy people *Osborne*
ISBN 0078821088

Eager, B (1996)
Using Internet with Windows 95: user friendly
reference *Que*
ISBN 0789704021

Gross, Michael (1995)
A pocket tour of law on the Internet *Sybex*
ISBN 0782117929

Hoffman, Paul (1995)
Netscape and WWW for dummies *IDG Books
Worldwide*
ISBN 1568843739
(NB will already be out of date as Netscape 2 has
now been released)

Levine, John R (1996)
Internet for dummies 3rd ed *IDG Books
Worldwide*
ISBN 1568846207

Rose, Lance (1995)
Netlaw: your rights in the online world *Osborne McGraw-Hill*
ISBN 0078820774 (US)

Schofield, Sue (1995)
The UK Internet book *Addison-Wesley*
ISBN 0201427664

Weiss, Aaron (1995)
The complete idiot's guide to downloading *Que*
ISBN 0789705672

4.7 Library Software

Requirements for software for legal libraries is little different from any other small special library. This is a selection of the most recent books:

Leeves, Juliet (1995)
Directory of library systems in the United Kingdom *Library Information Technology Centre*
ISBN 0951241281

Leeves, Juliet (1994)
Library systems in Europe: a directory and guide *TFPL*
ISBN 1870889479

Mansell, Robin (1994)
Management of information and communication technologies: emerging patterns of control *Aslib*
ISBN 0851423124

Rowley, Jennifer (1996)
Basics of information systems 2nd ed *Library Association Publishing*
ISBN 1846041360

Wright, Keith C (1995)
Computer related technologies in library operations *Gower*
ISBN 0566076322

Zeleznikow and Hunter (1994)
Building intelligent legal information systems *Kluwer*
ISBN 9065448330

4.8 Records Management

Central Computer and Telecommunications Agency (1994)
Requirements under the Public Records Act when using information technology *HMSO*
ISBN 011330630X

Diamond, SZ (1995)
Records management: a practical approach 3rd ed *AMACOM*
ISBN 081440295X

Gold, G (1995)
How to set up and implement a records management system *AMACOM*
ISBN 0814402925

Hendley, Tony and Broadhurst, Roger (1996)
Document management guide and yearbook 1996 *Cimtech*
ISBN 0900458720

Penn, IA (1994)
Records management handbook 2nd ed *Gower*
ISBN 0566075105

Wiegand, SA (1994)
Library records: a retention and confidentiality guide *Greenwood Press*
ISBN 0313284083

4.9 IT for Managers

Keen, PGW (1995)
Every manager's guide to information technology: a glossary of terms and concepts for today's business 2nd ed *Harvard Business School*
ISBN 08758475711 (US)

Wang, Charles B and Rothkopf, DJ (1994)
Techno vision: the executive's survival guide to understanding and managing information technology *McGraw-Hill*
ISBN 0070681554

INDEX TO ADVERTISERS